I0143509

FINDING GOD IN UNFAMILIAR PLACES

Stories of God's Grace and Mercy

BY
ROBERT LORAN FORD

All Rights Reserved @ Robert Loran Ford, 2020
His Way Publishing
Winston-Salem, North Carolina

ISBN: 978-0-9709580-4-4

DEDICATION

Throughout my journey in this world there have been many special events that have given new meaning to my life. I have over and over again been challenged to see the world from another perspective. This is certainly true with regard to my granddaughter, Taylor Loran Mosser. She came into our life on January 5, 2005, in Charlottesville, VA. A beautiful baby girl was placed before us, and we were all smitten by her. As we gazed upon her coming-into-the-world day, we were confronted with the mystery of what the future would be like for her.

Well, it has been fifteen years since that day in Charlottesville, and some of the mystery has been revealed. She has grown into a lovely young lady with personality plus. Like her grandfather Hobby (The nickname she gave me.), she has a great sense of humor and for the most part a rather easygoing way. There is spontaneity in her life that I find very refreshing and endearing. Yet, again somewhat like me, she has a shy component that could best be described as being thoughtful and reflective.

A master at navigating through a cellphone or an iPad, she has taught me so much about how to use these devices more efficiently, thus taking away some of the frustrations that were getting the better part of me. In other words, she has helped me to keep my sanity or at least to keep the little bit of sanity that still remains with me. In all of this, she has made me laugh and enjoy life. I find that she inspires all of us to live life to the fullest and to enjoy the company and presence of family.

So it is with great pride that I dedicate this book, *Finding God In Unfamiliar Places* to **Taylor Loran Mosser.**

ACKNOWLEDGMENTS

I am continually amazed at the responses I often get from folks who have read my first two books, *Behind Grandma's Apron Strings* and *Walking in Grandpa's Footsteps*. Somehow the stories make a connection with the lives of the readers. My stories come from various areas of life and circumstances. When I start writing I have no idea where I'm going with the line of thought, I just let it flow from my thoughts and life experiences, and most of all my imagination.

The encouragement of family and friends to write more has been a challenge and a blessing. I am challenged to dig deeper into my soul to find pieces of my life that I have left on the cutting room floor.

Nothing would have happened without the help of my longtime friend from college and seminary, Reverend Dennis Hester. Dennis and I stayed along with Jerry Burleson in the three upstairs rooms at Mrs. Hamrick's home in Lattimore, which was about ten miles from Gardner-Webb College (now University). Over the two years that I stayed there, we had some very lively discussions on theology, ethics, and biblical interpretation. It was this upper room experience that helped to sharpen my understanding of "Thus sayeth the Lord." To Dennis and Jerry I am deeply indebted for helping me establish a good foundation in my thought process.

In addition to all the hard work that Dennis has provided, I am also grateful for the expert editing provided by Rachael Garrity. She did such a professional job on the first two books that it was inevitable that she would be asked to provide her expertise to this book. Also, the technical support provided by All Tec Computer Service helped me through some areas that I couldn't seem to find my way through.

My family and friends still play an important role in the production of my books. Each time I say that I have written my last book, they insist that there is more books hidden somewhere inside me. Sure enough, they have been right.

My wife, Gail, has supported me throughout the process of all three books. I could not have asked for a better encouraging presence. My daughter, Lauran Gayle Ford Mosser, and my granddaughter, Taylor Loran Mosser, have both given me good feedback on my books. This is important because I have used stories from their lives throughout the books.

To all the above, I thank you from the bottom of my heart for your friendship and encouragement. Without you I would still be stuck in the mud of scrambled thoughts and ideas.

FOREWORD

Throughout our lives, each of us can remember incidents from our childhood that have impacted our adult lives. Some of us have said at one time or another, "I wish I had written down some of the things that happened in my life, because I could have learned some valuable lessons." Since most of us never take the time to record those events, they often fade into the recesses of our minds. On the other hand, Robert Loran Ford has taken the time to reach into his memories and recall the many events of his past that have impacted his life. He has found the hidden presence of God at work.

Robert has a dry sense of humor and a self-deprecating nature that come out in his retelling of how God's grace and mercy were evident throughout his life. As you read each vignette, you will find yourself reflecting on how God's grace and mercy have been evident in similar events on your journey through life. You, too, may come to realize how God has revealed Himself in the mundane events of your life.

I have had the pleasure of working alongside Robert as we try to help homeless and needy veterans in our community. At our weekly meeting, Robert ends each session with a short homily about how God works in our lives. All of us leave those meetings in a positive, hopeful frame of mind, thanks to Robert's insights on discovering God in unfamiliar places.

Read this book for the discoveries you may make, for the insights you may receive and just for the pure enjoyment of the God moments.

Dr. Ric Vandett
Retired School Superintendent
Colleague of Robert
Foothills Veterans Helping Veterans
Hickory, North Carolina

MESSAGE MENU

INTRODUCTION

The true value of an event is realized when it becomes a part of our memory. Each moment of our life has within it a piece of the puzzle of who we are and what our life is about. True, most of these moments are hidden in the recesses of our minds, but every now and then we remember a moment that invites us to stop and reflect. It is then that we may discover how God was present with us and we knew it not.

The ground of my theology is that God is always where God needs to be. We need not ask God to come into an event, because God is already there. What we need to do in these moments is to ask God to help us discover God's presence in the event.

My rendering of Revelation 3:20:

> Behold I stand at the door of your inner life and knock. If you are able to hear my knock and are willing to take the risk of opening the door, you will discover me. You will experience communion with me and me with you. You will discover the meaning of your life and your destiny. Please come in where I am already present and learn of me and discover yourself.

Again, our Lord is already where he needs to be. It is you and I who need to take a trip into our inner selves and discover the vastness of God's presence and God's activity within our lives.

In the following devotions, I have attempted to do this. It is a trip we cannot accomplish by our own efforts. We must have someone to help us discover all the pieces of our lives that we have left on the cutting room floor. It is these discarded pieces that hold so much meaning concerning who we are and the value of our lives. It is these pieces that tell a different story of our journey through life. Unfortunately, we live so close to the forest that we can't see the trees, so someone needs to help us.

The journey inward can be scary and filled with emotions that we have not felt before. With the help of family and friends, but mostly from other chaplain colleagues of mine, I have journeyed into unknown parts of my inner life. When events and times that I thought I had left behind began to come to the surface of my mind, it was painful for me. The fantasy of my life was being stripped away, and I became naked.

So, you see, the story of Adam and Eve is about hiding and discovery. To become naked before God and ourselves is not a good feeling. The natural thing to do is hide and hope that the discovery won't be made, but then along comes God, calling out to us to come out of our hiding place and discover God's love, grace, and mercy. This is what I have attempted to do in the following devotions. I hope and pray that you too will be willing to open the door and stand naked before God and discover that life is not all about what you have done or not done, but about what God has already done within your life. As we continue to allow ourselves to make this discovery, we are empowered and energized to live life to the fullest. To see and experience the world through the eyes of God gives us a whole new perspective of our world.

I invite you to come with me and be open to the present reality of God in some unfamiliar places of your life.

God's Grace,
Robert Loran Ford

A BIRD AFRAID OF HEIGHTS

Deep into the Smoky Mountains of Western North Carolina, in a tall oak tree, there lived the Robin Bird Family. They were a very beautiful family, with dark blue feathers and an orange undercoat. In the same tree, there lived the Redbird Family and the Blue Jay Family. Each family had taken time to build a nest just right for a family of five or six.

It was early spring, and soon it seemed that each nest had three or four eggs needing the full attention of the parents. This was the time of incubation when the parents would take turns nesting on the eggs to keep them warm. When the right time came, the small baby birds would hatch from the eggs. This would signal a frantic time of feeding the newborn birds in order for them to grow into strong adult birds of a feather.

With each new day, as bugs and other insects became more and more abundant, the feeding process became more successful. The expectations were high for the parents, as they watched their hatchlings grow and grow and grow. As this happened, the nest seemed to be getting smaller and smaller, until it became time for the little ones to expand their wings and flap them until the wings were strong enough to lift them into the air. This took a lot of practice, but each new day would find the young birds better equipped to lift off and leave the nest.

Eventually all the nests were empty, as the young birds found their way into the wild blue yonder. That is, all the nests were empty except for one, the home of Mr. and Mrs. Robin. They had hatched three eggs and now two of the three hatchlings were airborne. One lone young bird remained in the nest. His two siblings, R1 and R2, were gone to start their families. Only R3 remained.

In spite of numerous attempts by the parents to get the young bird to fly, he would not. He would go as far as the edge of the nest and look down and then jump back in complete horror. His home was high, high up in this giant oak tree. It must have been a distance of several hundred feet to the ground.

Every day, he would tell himself that today was the day. This was going to be the day that he would make his big jump into the adult world of birds. But as he reached the edge of the nest, and looked down, fear would grip his whole body. The thought of jumping out of a nest so high up terrified him. The pressure was on to follow his siblings into life's adventure, but he just couldn't make himself do it.

His parents wondered where they had gone wrong. Each day friends and family would stop by to see if the youngster had made his big jump into life. Each day they would see the youngster looking away from them with a sense of shame and disgust. He was a failure!

He was an embarrassment to his family who wanted him to succeed in life. But with each new passing day, it seemed to be getting more and more difficult for him to fly.

Questions ran through his mind. Why had the Great Bird in the Sky done this to him? Why couldn't he be like all the other birds and just do what he was supposed to be able to do? Why was he so afraid of heights? Real birds aren't afraid of heights. They soar above the trees. Height of flight has very little concern with functioning birds.

Unfortunately for R3, it was coming to the time of year when birds go wherever birds go. He would soon be left alone in his nest facing a do or die situation. His nest was falling apart bit by bit and would soon no longer be safe. The weather would be making a drastic change, and soon there would be snow covering the trees and the hillsides. With the leaves gone, the mountain winds would bring his nest down to the ground. It was time to do something or die. The choice was his.

It is in the midst of such crises that change is allowed to occur, bringing an openness that did not exist before and a willingness to take a risk. The mind is allowed to go places that had previously been off limits. This was one of those moments for R3. A light focused upon his tiny life that day, and a thought came to mind that empowered him to do what he did. The voice he heard seemed to say to him: "Trust what I have given you from birth. Trust the destiny I have set before you."

Call it an epiphany, a voice from the Great Spirit in the Sky. It was a voice more clear to him than any other voice he had ever heard. There was no mistake about what he needed to do, and now was the time to do it.

So R3 climbs to the edge of the nest, looks down and then looks up. He takes a deep breath and says, "YES," to the voice that had embraced him. Then he lets go. Without any thought, his wings begin their upward and downward motion. He can feel the wind beneath his wings and the thrust of life through the cool morning forest. He is moving at speeds he had never thought possible and executing maneuvers he had never dreamed he could do. Wow! What a life! It is unbelievable! When you respond to the Great Spirit in the sky, you discover a world full of possibilities and wonder.

We might say that R3 was reborn that day. There was a conversion in his life that put him on a new pathway. He discovered who he was and the meaning of his life. The sky and points beyond were his destiny. Soon he rejoined the company of family and friends and made his way with them off into the wild blue yonder.

It is from the Prophet Isaiah that we are encouraged to take flight. Those who face a great challenge in their lives, yet find a way to put their hope in God will discover new strength and a willingness to go forward. They will soar on the wings of eagles. They will run and not grow tired. They will walk, but not become weary. (*Paraphrase by RLF.*)

There is an old saying: "Nothing ventured, nothing gained." Life is full of risks that must be taken in order for us to experience our potential. We won't know unless we try. When God calls us to accomplish something, He provides a way for it to happen. There is always a mystery to the call of God. We are assured that God will never leave nor forsake us. The leap of faith is into the arms of God.

Are you ready to let go and let God?

CURTAIN, LIGHTS, ACTION

The "Tom Thumb Wedding" presented by the student body was the event of the year at Ruth Elementary School in Western North Carolina. While the school had the distinction of being the smallest school in the state, there were still somewhere in the neighborhood of 150 students, so there would be plenty of kids to play the various parts in the play. Somehow I became one of the kids selected, and my role would be "The Ring Bearer."

I can't remember how many practice sessions we had, but I do remember that on some occasions we had a practice session after lunch. My grandparents lived just down the road from the school, so I would go there for lunch from time to time. On this particular day, I remember telling Grandma I had changed my mind: I didn't want to be in the play. Grandma informed me that it was too late to back out now. I had to carry through with my commitment.

Still, I was not convinced that I should do this wedding thing. No! I had made up my mind and that was it. At about that time, we heard a knock on the door. Grandma opened the door to discover two girls sent to escort me back to school. It seems my reputation was well known by most of the teaching staff, who thought

9

I would probably bolt if given an opportunity. So off I went with these two classmates to fulfill my obligation. The whole school was waiting in the auditorium for me to arrive so that the practice session could continue. That accounted for all the mean looks I got.

It was my place to carry a white pillow with two rings firmly attached as a precaution, lest I somehow lose them. The rings belonged to the fifth-grade teacher, Mrs. Wilkens. As a last word of encouragement, she warned me that if I let anything happen to those rings, she would skin my head. At the time I had a decent head of hair, so I didn't need a skinned head. Wouldn't you know it? Even when I was a first-grader, my teachers knew me too well.

It was Saturday, May 2, 1952, and the auditorium was packed full with people who were desperate for entertainment. Well, you do need to take into consideration that TVs were few and far between in those days, so we had very little competition that Saturday night. Dressed in a white shirt and pants, I was anxious to get this thing over with and get on with my life. Then came the announcement, "Curtain, Lights, Action" and the show began.

From time to time, we become the chosen one whether we want to be or not. In fact, I would say that the sheer fact we are on this earth is an indication that we have been selected and called to something. There is a purpose in our being here, which we are to pursue. Your purpose is unique, so you are the only one who can carry it out. It cannot be given to someone else, because it is your special calling. You and you alone can complete this mission. Still, the question remains: "Are you willing to accept it?"

One day a man was about his daily chores when he heard a small whisper, a voice maybe from outside him, maybe from within, but he assuredly heard it. "I have a job for you. I want you to go to the place that I will show you. There you will deliver a message for me. Get up and prepare yourself for the journey."

"Where am I going? Can you at least tell me where you want me to go and what it is you want me to do?"

"That you will know in due time, but for now walk in the footsteps that I will show you," responded the Voice.

But again the man balked: "I don't think I want to go anywhere right now. I like things as they are, so you need to get someone else."

"No, you are the person for the job," the Voice replied. "I know who you are because I made you and formed you in your mother's womb."

"Maybe so," replied the man, "but I still don't want to go wherever you want me to go. While you may think I have the skills to accomplish this mission, I'm not so convinced. I can't see myself in that capacity. I don't perform well when it involves a lot of people, so you need to get someone who likes to do that kind of stuff. I know you have the right to send me, but I have the right to say 'No.' So, I'm not going! I wish you the best on finding someone for the job. I know there are a lot of folks to choose who will make you proud."

So off he went in his attempt to escape from this continual interruption of his life. One day as he was following some friends, he found himself in a military environment. He remained there for more than three years, and eventually circumstances led him back home, where he easily joined the daily life of his village and found a job that allowed him to live comfortably. With this the man was very satisfied! In fact, he thought that life couldn't get any better than this! What more could you want than to be left alone with no one wanting anything from you?

For the man, it was a blissful existence! But soon the winds of change came upon his life. A troubled mind came upon him with thoughts of the Voice that had bothered him so many years before. Again the man hears, "I need you to do this for me. I couldn't find anyone else in the whole wide world who could do it. I won't leave you alone until you answer my knock on your door."

Trying to defend himself, the man puts forth a deal that might get him off the hook: "I have one condition, and that one condition is that you get me into a school for the training that I need." The prophet, who barely escaped high school, knew that he would never be accepted into any school, so that would be the end of it.

One Saturday morning at a place set aside for testing one's ability in the academic world, the man poured over the vast number of questions. His high school days were far behind him, so there was a lot that he had forgotten, but he would do his best. When he had completed it, he went back home to continue his style of life. He would not be hearing from the Voice again, because this test would show once and for all that he was not the person who needed to be answering this call to a mission impossible.

After a few weeks went by, a letter with his name on it arrived in the mail. It contained the results of the test. As he opened the envelope, he knew that the score inside would nail the coffin shut. This would prove to the Voice how inept he would be for the job at hand. This was his way out, and the Voice would know just how incapable he was for the calling. The man tore open the letter, and as he ran his fingers down the page the unexpected happened. He was totally blindsided. How could this be? There must be some mistake! The score put him near the 1200 mark. The school he never thought would never accept him had received the report as well, and in another envelope was his acceptance.

The man had fought a good fight, but now he had to concede to the Voice. There was nothing left to do but follow in the footsteps before him and trust the one who would lead him. The years of following the Voice were fruitful. Doing what was thought to be impossible! Going far beyond what was thought possible, he stood amazed. How in the world could he have accomplished all of these things?

The journey of faith is born out of the mystery of the One who calls us and seeks to lead us to the land that will fill and define our destiny. In this journey we have the opportunity to discover who we are and what can be accomplished in our lives. We are called to take our place upon the stage, and to stand where the X is marked for us. We stand there not knowing the how or the where, but believing that the Voice will sustain us.

The stage is waiting for your arrival. The show cannot go on without you. You have a place there which no one else can fill. Do you hear the Voice?

Curtain, Lights, Action!

DIGGING IN THE DIRT

Excitement was filling the small community in the foothills of Western North Carolina. Gold had been discovered in California. The word was that in some parts of the hills the gold was just lying on top of the ground. John Henry Edwards was one of the young men struck by this dream of getting rich. He had come down with "gold fever." This whole frenzy had started when news arrived on January 24, 1848, that James W. Marshall had discovered gold at Sutter's Mill in Coloma, California. For many a man of that day, panning for gold beat farming by a long shot. For those already in California, it would be a rather short trip, but for those on the east side of the nation, it would be quite an adventure.

John Henry Edwards made his decision to go and seek his fortune. Kissing his wife and kids good-bye, he set out for St. Louis, MO, to connect with a wagon train going west. After a month or so, he had arrived safely and had high hopes of traveling with a group of like-minded dreamers. It was from St. Louis that the family received their first and last letter from him. He wrote that it was just a matter of getting there and getting the right gear and then heading for the hills. He expected to pan all the gold he would need in a few months, so in a short time he would be back home.

Mr. Edwards' intent was to find enough gold to provide for himself and his family. He could have the finer things of this world. He could own land and a big house and have people working for him, rather than being a sharecropper. Farming was not an easy endeavor. It certainly involved a lot of back-breaking work and long hours with rewards often taken away by a hot, dry summer.

Not many folks would have called the farming way of life easy in the mid 19th century. But it did have its reward. If things went well, the family could enjoy the fruits of their labor. There were three meals each day and time together that you couldn't put a price tag on. Perhaps, at some point in the early evening, sitting on your front porch with a cold glass of lemonade or iced tea, and feeling an occasional refreshing summer breeze going by, life seemed at its best! And if you had a comfortable rocking chair, it was even better. This is the peace and contentment that comes from God.

Still, Mr. Edwards wanted more out of life than he was getting. For him something was still missing, and the news of gold in California couldn't be resisted. He had to go and find his destiny. It would be a dangerous trip, but it would be worth it. This was a once in a lifetime opportunity that he could not and would not let go by. So off he went, never to be heard from again, but for one letter from St. Louis.

In the Book of Job, there is a chapter on Wisdom. It goes something like this:

There is a mine where silver is found, and a place where gold is refined. Iron is taken from the earth, and copper is melted from ore. Men light up the darkness, and search every recess. They break open a shaft far away from the people above, in places no foot has trodden. They swing to and fro on the ropes that lower them into the earth. Underneath they find the source of sapphires, and gold dust.

No bird knows of this place, no falcon's eye has seen it. No beast of the land trodden on it. Humans put the hammer to the flint; they excavate the mountains, cut out channels in the rock. Their eyes see the precious stones. They dam up the streams to pan for gold. What is hidden they bring to the surface.

But where can Wisdom be found? Where is the place for understanding? Humans do not have a clue about its value or where to find it. You will not find it at the marketplace among the living. If you go deep down into the earth, you will not find it. If you take a trip into the deepest recesses of the ocean, you will not find it. There is not enough gold or silver to purchase it. The price of Wisdom is above all precious jewels. From where then does Wisdom come, and where can understanding be found? It is hidden where no one can find it. It is concealed where no one can reveal it. But God understands its way, and He knows its place. God took a

good look in the mirror, and declared what
was seen to be Wisdom. God says to human
beings, the fear (the sense/awareness of the
otherness of God), is Wisdom, and to stop
doing bad things to ourselves and to others
is understanding. Job 28 (*Paraphrase by RLF*)

What are you digging for in life? Are you digging in
the right place? The Scripture says that we must each
work out our own salvation. Determining our destiny
is finding the answer to the question about what
purpose we were created to pursue? Some would say
that this is the call of God! Therefore, we get on the
right track by laying our lives open to God and inviting
God to bless us and to lead us in the way we should
go. The promise of God is if we seek, we will find.
Beyond finding, we need to know what to do with
what we have found.

The Wisdom of God is available to one and all. We
cannot find It; it finds us. The Good News is that the
hidden treasure is within us. It is not out there
somewhere in a faraway land. It is waiting to be
discovered within our lives.

The invitation is clear in Revelation 3:20, "Behold I
stand at the door and knock. If you will open the door
and come in I will reveal to you things concerning the
deeper meaning of your life." The traditional
understanding of this scripture is that our Lord is on
the outside wanting to come into our lives. I see it from
a different perspective. It is not our Lord on the
outside, but us. He is already where he needs to be. It

is you and I who need to come into the deeper recesses of our souls. I say this because I believe our Lord is always where He needs to be. He is the "Imigo Dei" (the image of God) which is within every human life. It was St. Augustine who once said, "To know God is to know self."

So I beg the questions:

Where Are You Digging?

and

"What Are You Digging For?"

ELLENBURG VS. FORD

We were just leaving our grandparents' home. We paused briefly on the front porch before stepping out into the pathway that led to my cousin's home, which was around 50 yards away. At first we just slowly made our way in that direction, but I knew what was coming. It was just a matter of time, and it would start as it had so many times before. No matter how hard I tried, I could not change the inevitable results. So, I took a deep breath in anticipation. At any moment I would hear Evelyn, my first cousin, blurt out: "I bet I'll beat you." So off we went running as fast as we could. She was fastest girl I had ever come up against. Over the years that we did this, I don't remember ever having beat her.

The Apostle Paul speaks of life as a race, which we all run at different speeds and in different directions. He writes in First Corinthians 9: 24-25:

> Know ye not that they which run in a race run all, but one receives the prize? So run, that ye may obtain. And every person that strives for the mastery is temperate in all things. Now they do it to obtain a corruptible crown; but we an incorruptible. (*KJV*)

To put Paul's thought in a nutshell, there are some things that come and go like the weather. They don't last. They have a short shelf life. But there are some things that have eternal significance. These things go beyond the grave. They live on in eternity.

This is not to say that there is anything wrong with competition. Competition brings out the best in us and prepares us for the greater challenges ahead. Paul in a subtle way presses the thought that we need to be aware of where we are running to and for what reason. In a song by Peggy Lee, she asks the question "Is this all there is to life?" A life well spent is a life that finds its goal in God.

Evelyn and I ran our race just for the fun of it, but there comes a time in every person's life at which some decision is made as to what in the world is worthy of pursuit. This choice is made either with some thought process or with little or no thought process. We may choose just to drift through life or we may want to be more intentional about the direction our life is taking. As the years have gone by, Evelyn and I have taken different pathways in life, but the connection is still there. I still have the letters she wrote to me when she went away to Bible College in Ohio. She was concerned about my relationship with God. She prayed for me and encouraged me to be the person God wanted me to be. I have no doubt that she played a big part in my transformation. I played the part of the prodigal. I went to the far country, running after what I thought was of great value. I was good at running with the crowd without much thought of where we were going. My years in the Air Force had perfected some bad habits in my life, which I brought home with me. I was still wild as a buck.

Evelyn continued to pray for me to find a deeper relationship with God. At one point, I was at a local fast food restaurant with Evelyn's husband, Veon. Pointing out a group of men who were apparently under the influence of alcohol, making fools of themselves, he said: "Well, the devil doesn't have to worry about those guys; he already has them in his back pocket."

His words hit me right between the eyes. Right then and there I knew that I had to make some changes in my life. I was running the race to nowhere. So from that point on, I started getting back with the people who could help me get my life straightened out. I started going to church again and was there every time the doors were open. I started reading my Bible that was given to me at my high school graduation. I started having a devotional life and a prayer time in my daily schedule. Eventually, I answered God's call for me in ministry. This was the race that I needed to be in, and it felt good and wholesome to me.

I was fortunate to have a cousin who cared deeply about my relationship with God and the direction that my life was going at the time. Evelyn's prayers helped me to make my way back home to be embraced by God. You see, Evelyn knew what the race was all about and she wanted me to run with her.

What race are you running?

ESCAPING THE PIGPEN

The Prodigal left home looking for a home! He thought he would find home in the far country, only to discover how barren his life was. His core sin was living as though he had no home. So he had to leave home to find home! As one of the songs in the play "Into the Woods" says: "He ventured out and found himself."

The Gospel according to John Chapter 15 has Jesus' discourse to His disciples. He tells them that in His Father's House there are many rooms, that He goes to prepare a place for them and that He will return, so that they may be with Him there in the Father's House.

This scripture is more often than not interpreted as relating to the future, to a day far, far away. I believe that it has a more earthly meaning. It was a reminder to his disciples that they were to live their lives as "children of God" who belong to His household. Wherever their life experiences might take them, whatever might be required of them, they were to live as "children of the Father."

The sin of the Prodigal was that he lived as though he had no home, no room, no Father. This self-perception had left him barren in a foreign land. It took going to the "pigpen" to bring him to his senses. It was his "teachable moment." The turning point for the Prodigal Son came in a "pigpen" far away from home.

His journey to the far country had left him barren. No family, no home, no food, no hope!

His life experience coincided with his world view-- "a famine arose in the far country." The question arises: Is there any way out of the pigpen? Consider: "He came to his senses." Evidently, he was not alone in the pigpen, as Daniel was not alone in the lion's den. So Someone was present with the Prodigal.

The purpose of the Book of Genesis, which was written sometime during and after the Post-Exilic Period in Israel's history, was to give hope to the people of God having a "pigpen" experience in life. Some of the people had been taken from their homeland, while others had been left back home among the destruction and ruins of a demolished city and nation, with foreign occupation all around. They begged the questions: Can anything overcome all this chaos? Can our nation ever be recovered? Is there any hope for us?

The Creation Story is directed toward this life situation of God's people. The message is this: The God Who moved across the chaos in the beginning and brought forth all life is the same God Who will overcome our "pigpen" experience and will bring forth new life.

The Good News is that there is hope beyond our "pig-pen" experience of life. Home is really not that far away. Our Father's home is waiting for our arrival. Our room is ready for occupancy. While Dorothy had to tap her shoes three times to get back to Kansas, you only need to say, "God be merciful to me, a lost soul who needs to come home to you."

The scripture reminds us that if we seek, we will find, and that if we ask, it will be given. As the old hymn puts it, what our Father has done for His other children, He will do for you. With arms wide open, He will welcome you back home.

So what do you say? Are you ready to come back home?

FROM WICHITA TO L.A.

Here I sat in the belly of a C-141 on its way to George AFB in California. Passenger seats had been installed to accommodate all the staff involved in this tour of duty. My specialty was navigation. In my previous years with the Air Force, I had worked on the navigational systems of C-124's, C-130's, C-141's, RF-4C's, and F-105's. Each plane had its own unique guidance system to ensure arrival at the right place and hopefully a return flight back to point "A".

On this flight there was no stewardess walking around taking our request for drinks or snacks. No, this an Air Force no thrills, nonstop flight from McConnell AFB in Wichita, Kansas, to George AFB located near L.A. The flight out was a little bumpy, and the metal seats did not make for a comfortable trip. With not a lot to do, I decided to go up to the cockpit and check out how the navigational system was working. The C-141 had several systems, so I curious as to which one was being used to get us to our destination.

In the cockpit there was the pilot and co-pilot and the navigator. After introducing myself, I asked how the navigational system was working. To my surprise the navigator informed me that he had it turned off. "Turned off," I exclaimed, "then how are we navigating this trip?"

"Take a good look at the pilot," was the navigator's response. That was strange. What was he doing looking out the window?

At this point the pilot's voice kicked in, "Dead reckoning!"

"Are you kidding me," I responded.

"No," was his response. "We are following the interstate highway that will lead us to our target."

Sure enough that was what the pilot was doing. Just following the highway down below to California. It seems that all the navigational equipment was wasted on this plane. If we had flown into a storm on our way, then the system of navigation might have changed. Fortunately for us, that didn't happen. We arrived at George AFB without any problems.
The F-105s from McConnell had already arrived, so all that was left for us worker-bees to do was to find our workplace and our housing for this TDY (Temporary Duty).

It was a good four months of duty. It seems that the pilots of the F-105's used their navigational systems like the pilot on our C-141: never. This meant that there were work orders being generated by the pilots, so nothing for us navigational specialists to do but have fun. We came into our workplace on Mondays and Fridays to check and see if by chance some pilot had accidently turned on one of the navigational systems to discover that it wasn't working. It never happened. So no complaints from me.

You know, there is a difference between knowing you have a guidance system and deciding not to use it, and having a guidance system and not knowing you have one. First Kings 22:4 records a visit between the kings of the northern and southern kingdoms. King Ahab of Israel and King Jehoshaphat of Judah are discussing war issues. Ahab asks Jehoshaphat if he would be willing to help him. Jehoshaphat's answer is: "Before you do anything, ask God for guidance."

A good piece of advice for any of us thinking about starting a war with someone. Who would argue the point that there is entirely too much violence in our world? I would add that we have too much violence that did not start with asking God for guidance.

As I write this, I do so as violence spreads across our nation like a thick fog. Mr. George Floyd was murdered by four Minneapolis police officers. He was already handcuffed for allegedly passing a counterfeit $20 bill. They put him on the ground, and one police officer put his knee on Mr. Floyd's neck for eight minutes. During this time Mr. Floyd cried out that he could not breathe, but the officer would not stop and continued to apply the pressure. Eventually Mr. Floyd went limp and died. Again, this incident has become the spark that caused a wildfire to spread across our country. It should never have happened, but it did.

I would like to think that it will never happen again, but it will. The writer of Second Chronicles writes that many of God's people are seeking advice from the wrong place. By doing so they are getting bad guidance on how to navigate life. To this God says, "You will become a bad joke among the peoples of the world." When tourists come through your land they will ask, "What happened here? What's the story behind these ruins?"

So who is guiding your life?

GOING NORTH ON I-77

It was a Saturday, I believe, when my first cousin, Wayne Ford, and his family decided to make a trip up Interstate Highway 77 into the wild country of West Virginia and points beyond. Once you get beyond the North Carolina state line, the road gets a little hilly with a lot of curves. I have been up that road on several occasions, and the view from up there is spectacular. At points you can see for miles and miles as the tree line drops off to reveal the scenic Shenandoah Valley.

During the Civil War this place was a hell hole, but today it is the picture of tranquility.

So as time goes by, it becomes time for a pit stop, popularly known as a restroom break. It came to a point that Wayne just couldn't wait any longer, so he pulled the car over to the side of the road, and hopped out to find a good place to relieve himself. Some small bushes were just a few feet away from the car, so Wayne made a beeline for them to find some cover. Rather than just pass through between the bushes, he took a giant leap over the top.

The rest of the family waited patiently in the car for Wayne's return. Ten or fifteen minutes went by, but the family was not alarmed, figuring that Wayne needed just a little more time. Eventually the 10 to 15 minutes turned into 30 and then 45 minutes and still no Wayne in sight. Not wanting to embarrass him by going through the bushes to discover what was going on, the family remained seated in the car, believing that Wayne would show up at any minute.

It had been close to an hour when in the distance there was some rustling of the bushes, and then Wayne appeared. There was something different about him on his return to the car. His clothing had some tears and a shoe was missing, along with scratches on his arms and face. What in God's name had happened to him? they wondered.

Back in the car, Wayne explained his ordeal. It seems that the small bushes he leaped over in a single bound were more than bushes. They were the tops of trees growing along the highway far down below. He had fallen some twenty or thirty feet down through these trees and finally landed. His restroom needs were probably performed on his way down, so the rest of the time was spent trying to figure out how to get back up the almost vertical cliff.

Thankful that there were no broken bones, just a few scratches here and there, Wayne and his family continued their adventure up I-77. I'm sure this episode dominated the conversation for many days and weeks to come. Probably a lesson that Wayne would like to forget, but it had become part of the family legacy and would never go away.

Assuming that the bushes were just that, bushes, when they were instead treetops nearly cost Wayne his life. I have made a lot of assumptions in my life. I have assumed that the person talking with me was telling me the truth. I have assumed that a friend was honest and would do the right thing. I have assumed that people would do what they said they were going to do. I have assumed that a friend I loaned money to would pay me back. I have assumed that a friend would not steal from me. I have assumed that people would not tell lies on me for no good reason. I have assumed that if I treat people right that they will treat me right. My assumptions go on and on, and so do my disappointments.

You see, I'm a trusting soul. I believe that people are good until proven otherwise. Do I get hurt a lot? Yes, I do! Do I get angry at myself for being so naïve? Yes, I do! Do I wish at times that I wasn't so trusting? Yes, I do! I have given much thought to this and here is what I have decided. I have a choice in the matter. I can let others decide who I am or I can let the mind of Christ determine who I am.

In one of his letters, the Apostle Paul writes; "Let the attitude/mind of Christ be in you." In His Sermon on the Mount, Jesus spoke of those who hurt us and do all matter of things against us. Usually they are people we think we know, so we let our guard down, only to find out that these persons were not who we thought they were. This happens in a variety of relationships, and it happens over and over again. I can't count the number of fights I've witnessed between two guys fighting over a girl. Not me! If a person doesn't want me around or likes someone else better, so be it. There are plenty more relationships available; it's just the matter of finding the right person.

So I refuse to let how people treat me determine how I respond. In the old wild west days, the "solution" was to go out into the street and have a shootout. Fastest man wins! That's not my style! As scripture says, "Vengeance is mine says the Lord."

So does this mean that I should keep letting the same person do me in over and over? No! I remind friends to whom I've loaned money that they still have an outstanding debt to me. So I don't throw good money after bad. I cut my losses and go on with my life.

I refuse to let my misplaced assumptions about people make me into an angry, vengeful person. That's not who I am. Life is too short to for me to waste my time and energy hating someone, and then spend the rest of my life trying to figure out how to get back at them. I tell you, it's a waste of time, and most important, it's a waste of your life. Life is too short for this kind of stuff. I like to live free from the bad restraints that the desire for revenge places upon me. It's hard to soar with eagles with all this stuff wrapped around you.

Bottom line, I will continue to make some assumptions out of good faith in my fellow man or woman. I will get hurt again! But I will enjoy my life to the fullest. I will not imprison myself with bad thoughts of other people, even those who have hurt me. No, I'm not going to do it.

So the choice is yours! Become a person who believes everybody is out to get you and decide not to trust anyone any more or choose to let the attitude/mind of Christ to be in you and to control your thoughts and actions.

Who are you?

GUESS WHO'S COMING
TO DINNER

They lived on the other side of the small patch of woods near my home. Quite curious as to what was going on over there, I made my way in that direction. There was a small restaurant and several homes scattered throughout the village. In one shop a lady was making a garment. Her sewing machine kept up a steady pace as the needle made its way across the formless cloth. She moved a paddle underneath the machine back and forth with her foot, causing the needle to move up and down and eventually a new shirt or blouse would be completed. Some lucky person would be wearing a new shirt tomorrow.

At another place, there was a small porch with a rocking chair (my favorite kind of chair) and a gentleman by the name of Uncle Merritt. He spoke to me first, and invited me to come up on the porch and join him. I started to tell him my name, but he stopped me dead in my tracks. "I know who you are and I know your parents," he said.

Boy, I didn't expect that, so I just finished my way to the porch and the rocking chair waiting for me. We talked as we rocked until Uncle Merritt took a look at his pocket-watch and announced that it was time for lunch. "You will be staying for lunch won't you, Mr. Ford?" It seemed like a good offer to me.

I believe the entire village came to Uncle Merritt's place for lunch. He could not walk for some reason, so he moved about in a wheelchair. At the table, they put me between Uncle Merritt and Aunt Dosey, his wife. As I looked around the table, I noticed that I was the only white person there. I later discovered that this small village was the home of the black mill hands who worked at Grace Cotton Mill where my father worked.

They were good people and always invited me to lunch when I was around. I was treated like one of the family and that felt good to me. The fact that they all knew my name was amazing, and since they also knew my love of rocking chairs, the one on the porch was always available for me. Over the years that we lived in the little house near the woods, I made many trips to visit my friends in the village. The hospitality was always the same, "Well, Mr. Ford, would you like to have lunch with us today?"

The Gospel according to Matthew provides an excellent view of the table fellowship of the historical Jesus, which was a hard pill to swallow for some of the upper crust of the community. The Jesus that Matthew presented to his people was one who ate with outcasts, the unclean, tax collectors, and the godless heathens of the world.

On the night before He was crucified, Jesus met with his disciples for a meal. He broke bread and drank wine with his disciples and announced that he was giving them a new commandment (Maundy Thursday). Since then, the Christian Church celebrates what is called Communion. When Jesus celebrated it that night, it was a full meal, but today churches celebrate it with wine and bread.

Its purpose is fellowship. In the celebration, God communes with his people. His presence blows upon and across his people. God is present. God is active. The experience of fellowship with God is both a present reality and a promise of the coming reality of God. God has come into the life of his people, God is coming into the life of his people, and God will continually come into the life of his people. Table fellowship with God is both promise and fulfillment. It is both present and future.

Why do we say "grace" before a meal? Most would say to thank God for the food. It's more than this. Every meal is communion. Every meal is fellowship. More important than the food before us is the presence of God that surrounds us and dwells within us. These special occasions with family and friends provide a doorway, an opportunity to experience fellowship with God through our relationships. God meets us in these mundane events of life, as well as in the Holy Communion. As such, we feast upon God. While taking of the Sacrament takes only a few minutes, the Feasting never ends.

With every breath we take we breathe in the "Ruah," which from the Old Testament means Wind or Spirit of God. The breeze that makes its way across our face contains the "Ruah." With each and every beat of our heart we pump the life-giving blood, which contains the Presence of God within us. Our bodies continue to tell us of the ongoing Presence and work of God. And when death comes, as with Enoch, God takes us! The Divine Feasting goes on for Eternity.

The fact that we are alive is testimony that God exists in us, for all life is from God and is sustained by God. This thought is not "Pantheism," but more correctly "Pan-In-Theism. The former thought is that God is a certain object or thing. The latter term describes God as being in all things, but not being the thing itself.

I believe that God is always where He needs to be. It is we human beings who need to get into the life of God. We are the people coming to dinner. God is already there and calling us to join Him in the Feast of Family. Because God is in us and we are in Him, to take God into our lives is also to take all who are in God into our lives. So, in a broader perspective, in Holy Communion we feast upon God and God's family as well. We are brought into a Holy Brother and Sisterhood. The Holy Meal accomplishes what we cannot do by our efforts, but is accomplished by God.

Thus this is the meaning behind the Divine Invitation found throughout Scriptures. "Come eat of my food and drink my wine." Proverbs 9:5 (*Paraphrase by RLF*) So, "Whether you eat or drink or whatever you do, do for and to the glory of God." I Corinthians 10:31 (Paraphrase by RLF)

God invites you to have a meal with him, will you be there?

HEALING WORDS

Henry had been coming to the VHV (Veterans Helping Veterans) weekly meeting for several months, when he explained to the group that he was approaching the time when his stay at the Salvation Army would have to end. (He had previously been living in the woods.) After the meeting, he asked Chaplain Ford if they might talk some more about what was going on in his life. I had time, so we sit down on the sofa in the Upper Room as it was called at Grace House, a place where people from all sorts of life situations came during the day. The conversation went something like this:

Chaplain: Henry, what is it that you would like to talk about?

Henry: Well, I really don't know where to start.

Chaplain: Start anywhere you want to, that will be fine with me.

Henry: Well, I grew up in Maryland until I was eight years old, and then my parents got a divorce, and then I had to go live with some relatives that I don't believe wanted me anyway.

40

Chaplain: What makes you think they did not want you?

Henry: Well, they kind of blamed me for putting the family under a lot of hardship financially.

Chaplain: How did you handle that?

Henry: Not good! I hated being a burden on them. My cousins would blame me if they did not get what they wanted from their parents. Said that I was just a big drain on the family and that's why they couldn't ever go anywhere nor do anything.

Chaplain: How did you deal with that?

Henry: Well, I felt bad about it and I wished that I could be somewhere else where I was wanted.

Chaplain: If you could have been somewhere else, where would you want to be?

Henry: Well, I would have liked to be back with my parents, but I knew that was not going to happen. So as I got older, I started doing a little drinking, and a few drugs here and there, until it became a problem at school and I was suspended permanently. At that time my relatives sent me off to some sort of reform school, and I never heard from them again.

Chaplain: Did you miss hearing from your relatives?

Henry: Not really. At least I didn't have to listen to the family sitting around and blaming me for all their troubles.

Chaplain: Was the reform school any better?

Henry: Well, not a lot better than it was at my relatives' place. People were still mean to me, and I would catch hell if anything went wrong.

Chaplain: Why do you think people do not like you?

Henry: Well, I think because wherever I go, things just go bad, and I'm the cause of it.

Chaplain: What is it about you that cause things to go bad?

Henry: Well, I think that I'm just a screw-up. I'm what they call a 'bad seed.' Some people are meant to do good things, and some of us are just meant to do and cause bad things to happen.

Chaplain: Tell me about something good you have done in your life.

Henry: That's a difficult question. I can't think of anything. No I don't believe that anything good has ever come out of me. If it has, nobody told me about it.

Chaplain: Is there anything good going on in your life today?

Henry: No, I don't know of anything. I'm out of work, don't have a place to stay, and well, I am here, so I guess this is something good for me, but I don't see that I'm any help to anybody here or that I'm doing anything to pay my way, so I'm still just a person who takes, and gives nothing back. That's not good for the others. I don't have anything to give to nobody, and if I did they wouldn't want it.

Chaplain: If you could give something back to others, what would it be?

Henry: I don't know. . . I've never had anything to give back. . . I don't know.

Chaplain: What is it that you missed about your parents that you never got from your relatives, and never got from reform school or group home?

Henry: Just being wanted and knowing that somebody cared for me.

Chaplain: And have you felt wanted or cared for by anybody in the VHV Group?

Henry: Yes I have! I have made some friends here. You know this is not my family, but in a way it is family, ain't it?

Chaplain: Is that how you have experienced this group over the several weeks that you have attended our meetings?

Henry: Yes, it is, because there is something here that I've been looking for, but did not know where to find it. There is something here that keeps drawing me back again and again. I leave here with some good feelings about folks having an interest in what's going on in my life. Yes, this is something good in my life. This is very good, and I can't believe that I have stumbled upon such a group of people. Hell, I don't even know how I got here! I was trying to find the "Soup Kitchen" to get a meal and ended up here. Boy, what a lucky thing for me!

Summary:
The "good stuff" of Henry's story lay on the cutting room floor. We so often do this to ourselves. We seem to think that these bits and pieces of our lives don't matter and aren't worth very much, but if we allow ourselves to reach down and pick up some of these pieces of our lives and re-examine them, we may find pieces of gold and silver. As I walked with him through his story, he discovered on his own that there was something good about his life. This bit of understanding was life-changing for Henry. His life went from "gloom and doom" to "hope and expectation." We helped him find work and a place to live. Because he is a veteran, there were a number of benefits available to him. There came a day when we didn't see Henry at our meetings. He had taken wings of an eagle, and was now engaged in building a new life for himself.

From the prophet Isaiah, we have these words:

44

> Those who wait upon the Lord will get new strength. They will experience the uplifting life that God brings. They will soar like Eagles. They will run, but not grow tired of life. They will continue their journey, but not grow weary. Isaiah 40:31 (*Paraphrase by RLF*)

I suppose that most of us have had our share of bad times, when it seemed that everything was going wrong and nothing was going right. It is easy to get down on ourselves as we carry the burdens of the world upon our shoulders. At some point we may hear a call, a summons from a direction we were not expecting. It may sound something like this:

> Come unto me all you that carry heavy burdens in your life, and I will give you rest. Take the yoke that I have made especially for you and you will discover what I can do for you. I will only give you what you can manage in life. Knowing me, you will find rest for your soul. For my yoke fits you to a tee and your burdens will feel much lighter. Matthew 11:31 (*Paraphrase by RLF*)

God is always about the business of guiding us from where we are to where we need to be.
Do you hear the call?

HEART FAILURE

It was January. The snow was beginning to fall as I drove north on I-85 toward Hickory, N.C. The Army Chaplains' Conference in Atlanta, GA, had been a good one, but now it was time to make the trip back home. As the snow increased in intensity, I was hoping to at least make it to Spartanburg, SC, where my parents lived. What was normally a 3½- to 4-hour trip was becoming a 6- to 7-hour trip. I would be lucky to make Spartanburg before nightfall. Eventually I pulled into my parents' driveway with a sigh of relief. I had made the trip to this point safe and sound.

I called my wife to let her know that I was ok and would be spending the night with my parents. Mom provided a good, hot meal, and as we talked my father complained of having a lot of indigestion. A bottle full of Tums was no help. I encouraged him to see a doctor if the symptoms did not go away.

The next day, I was off to Hickory and made the trip without incident. A few days later I received a call from my mom that Dad was in the hospital with an apparent heart attack. It seems that all that discom-fort he had experienced was a heart attack coming on. He had put off getting medical help for as long as he could, but his delayed response had resulted in a significant amount of heart damage. He was 64 and scheduled to retire in 6 months. It never happened! The last 4 months of his life was one episode of heart failure after another. He had waited too late to get help, and it cost him his life. I was really upset with him for not taking better care of himself.

Heart failure is not something you want to have. The muscles of the heart have been damaged by lack of blood flow which cannot be reversed. For some folks with this health issue, a heart transplant is the only cure. This was the case with my uncle, Herman Tony. He lived a long productive life after his surgery and was thankful every day for his opportunity to enjoy life.

The prophet Ezekiel was taken captive by the Neo Babylonian Army, which had defeated the Southern Kingdom of Judah. He, along with many others, was transported to the Kingdom of Babylon. In a foreign land, which offered little or no hope of a meaningful life, Ezekiel preaches a positive message. He says to his fellow captives:

> Thus saith the Lord, I will give you a new heart and I will put a new spirit within you; I will remove your heart of stone from your flesh and I will give you a new heart of flesh. Ezekiel 36:26 (*Paraphrase by RLF*)

A "heart of stone," what would that look like? To say the least, it would be a dysfunctional heart. In that day and time, the heart was thought to be the center of love and compassion. A heart of stone could not love self, neighbor, or God. It could not enter into a meaningful relationship. It would not have the capacity to feel the touch of a loving, caring person. It would not have the capacity to know and feel the touch of God upon its life. The updated version of this concept would be a person who has no heart. To be heartless is to live a life without compassion.

In the movie, "The Wizard of Oz," the Tin Man complained that he had no heart. He would bang on the outside and from within could be heard a hallow sound. The assumption was that there was nothing inside, but coming events proved that indeed he had a big heart. He just didn't realize it. We all are made in the "image of God." This means we all have the capacity to love and be loved and to have compassion, if we so desire. If our hearts are filled with bitterness and hatred, we will build a wall around our lives to shut out the world around us. We will only associate with "birds of a feather." As Edwin Markham once wrote:

> He drew a circle to shut me out.
> Heretic, rebel a thing to flout!
> But love and I had a wit to win,
> we drew a circle that took him in.

While we can reject God by shutting Him out, God has drawn a circle to take us in. So like the Tin Man who thought he had no heart, you may one day discover your life has more potential than you realize.

If you are having spiritual heart problems, you need to make an appointment with the Great Physician, who is able to turn your heart of stone into a heart that can feel the touch and presence of God.

Are you ready to make this visit?

HI! HO! SILVER!

It was a Friday afternoon in the early fall of 1963, and I was on my way to Chester, SC, with my friend, Johnny Strickland. Johnny was the kind of person who never met a stranger, so at some point in our journey at Spartanburg TEC, our paths had crossed. We lived not too far apart and Johnny had asked me to come to home with him in Chester. He mentioned that we could ride his uncle's horses, which sounded like a good idea to me. Although I had never ridden a horse before, I was willing to give it a try. Also, Johnny told me he had a younger sister, which also sounded good to me. So it seemed that this trip to Chester could turn into a very interesting adventure.

The next morning found us out at the stables trying to decide which horse would be best for me. I eventually ended up with the smaller horse, which was supposed to be user friendly. Unfortunately, it turned out otherwise. The horse never missed a chance to knock me off by running so close to a tree that I would have to do a Wild Bill Show maneuver or alternatively running under a low limb on a tree, which meant I would have to hide behind one side of his head. Remember I had never ridden a horse before, so this was all new to me. I had to go into the survival mode in order to come back to the stables in one piece.

Eventually, after I thought I had the horse figured out, Johnny and I were racing down a rural highway and this "user-friendly" beast decided to go down an embankment and came to an abrupt stop at the bottom. Everything connected to the horse came to a sudden stop except me. I found myself airborne, having been propelled over his head, and soon made an ugly landing.

When I agreed to ride horses with my friend from Chester, I never knew what challenges that would bring my way and how close I would come to getting hurt. In other words, I did not count the cost of my decision to ride a horse. There were a number of times that morning that I thought I had bitten off more than I could chew, but by the grace of God I made it safe and sound.

When Jesus had numerous people indicate they wanted to "ride his horse," he was careful to inform them that the experience would not be easy. In the Gospel according to Luke, Chapter Nine and starting with verse 57, three different individuals approached Jesus about riding along with him on his journey, but were told they needed to count the cost of their decisions. One would need to go sell all he had, because the weight of all his stuff would be too much for the horse. Another decided he needed to go home and put things in order, which meant that the horse would probably be dead by the time he made his way back. Still another needed to go home and bury his father, who was not dead and probably nowhere near being dead. Again by the time he came back, the horse would be dead. Each of these three men who at first said they wanted to ride with Jesus, changed their minds. It was their "Hi Ho Silver Moment" opportunity, but when confronted with the horse of Jesus, they decided not to ride.

In short, it is rather easy to get on the horse of Jesus, but it is another thing to ride off with all the demands such an action requires. It is one thing to have dreams of a Hi Ho Silver Moment with Jesus, but it is another thing to make that dream come true.
Which are you? A dreamer or a doer!

MARBLES AND GOLF

Every morning it was the same routine: eat my breakfast and let Mom wash behind my ears before I went out the door to go to Ruth Elementary School. But there was one other item in my routine, and that was to put ten marbles in my pocket, plus one shooter. You see, the game of marbles was a big item at school. Those of us who arrived early would spend our free time down on the playground "shooting marbles," as it was called.

There were several different ways the game could be played, but the most popular seemed to be drawing a square in the dirt and into which each player would put in an equal number of marbles. There was no limit to the number of players or the number of marbles placed in the square. As the participants grew, so did the size of the square.

The next step was to draw a straight line in the dirt. Each player would shoot at the line with a marble, and the person who shot his marble closest to the line got to go first. From that same line each participant would shoot a marble at the marbles in the square. You got to keep all the marbles you knocked out of the square. If your shooter marble did not come out of the square, you were out of the game, and you had to put all the marbles you had knocked out back into the square.

I don't know if being left-handed had anything to do with it, but marbles was a game I was very good at. I would go to school with ten marbles and come back home with somewhere between 50 and 100. In fact, my success meant no one wanted to play marbles with me. So I switched games.

In another popular game, each participant would place an equal number of marbles inside a large circle. Again, the order of shooting was determined by rolling your shooter marble toward a straight line. Whoever was closer went first and then the next closest went second and so on and so on. The marbles were placed in the center of the circle, closely packed together. The challenge was to knock one of the marbles out of the circle without leaving your shooter marble inside the circle. If that happened, you were out of the game and all marbles you had knocked out previously would have to be put back into the circle.

Again, I was very good at this game and eventually no one would play with me. So I went to another game involving an old cigar box with a hole in the top just a little bigger than an average marble. Players dropped a marble from waist level toward the hole. Every marble that did not go through the hole, I got to keep. When a marble went through, I had to give the person five or ten marbles, which ever had been agreed upon at the time. Eventually I was banned from this game too, so I just quit playing marbles. At home I had more than twenty coffee cans full of marbles, so I really did not need any more.

I have long ago left marbles behind and have now moved into a more challenging game called "golf." Some days out on the golf course I wish I were still playing marbles. The game of golf still eludes me, yet it entices to come back again and again. Some people watching me play would say that I'm a glutton for punishment.

Here's the connection that I have come up with concerning marbles and golf. In both games there are rules each player is expected to follow. While Jesus probably never played a game of marbles or golf, he did know something about the game of life. Wherever he saw people not playing by the rules, he would let them know about it.

The woman caught in the act of adultery was condemned to die, that was the rule, but Jesus let it be known that there was another rule that trumped her death sentence, and that was God's grace and mercy and forgiveness and acceptance of all people, good or bad. The men of the village were ready to stone the adulteress, but Jesus reminded them that they, too, were sinners in need of the grace of God. It must have been a painful revelation, because each of the accusers walked away, dropping their stones as they went.

The Ten Commandments have been around a long, long time. At the top of the list is to love God and to obey God in worship and in life. When Jesus came along and preached his Sermon on the Mount as found in the Gospels of Matthew and Luke, he added that you should love God with all your heart, mind, and soul and your neighbor as yourself.

This led some to ask, "Who is my neighbor?" Good question! Jesus answered with a story about a good Samaritan. You have to realize that in that day and time there was no such thing as a good Samaritan. A lot of people in the time of Jesus considered Samaritans to be at the bottom of the humanity totem pole. Yet Jesus tells a story of a Samaritan who does a good deed for another human being in need of help. Bottom line, in God's rules of life there is no hierarchy of humanity. Rich or poor, whichever the case may be, "God so loves the world, the whole world, every person in the world, regardless of race or religion."

In the game of life, whose rules are you using?

MEAN AS A SNAKE

(The opening of this devotion is taken from a viewpoint of a resident snake and an intruder snake. It is taken from the animal world, not the human world. The point is that we can learn from the animal world how to play the game of life fairly without killing one another.)

His kingdom surrounded his home, which had been passed down to him through many generations. He was not about to give it up to an intruder. Closely he watched as the unwelcome one made his way across the property. Maybe he would just go on through without incident. But that was not likely to happen! This was choice property and a very good source of food and shelter. No, you wouldn't find a place like this anywhere else.

He realized that when you have something that everybody wants, you have to fight to keep it or you will lose it. He was always armed with his trusty weapon just in case of intrusions. Sure enough, it looked as if the intruder, realizing the value of the property, decided he would stay for a while. So a showdown was in the making. He would need to confront this and send him on his merry way.

Taking a closer look at the stranger, he saw a competitor just as big and ferocious as he was. This fight might take some time, but it had to be done. Slowly he moved from his vantage point, aware that he had a couple of options. He could do this at a slow pace or he could stage an ambush. Taking a deep breath, he made his move. Fast and furious he wrapped his body around the still unsuspecting invader and slammed him to the ground. But the guy bounced back up, ready to go at it again.

The posturing continued as did the relentless struggle for superiority. Who would tire first? Death was always a possibility, but not likely. Both participants had the capacity to inflict a deadly wound, but neither would do it. The refusal to do so had a long history among combatants like these two, so it was kind of ingrained into their being to avoid the death blow.
Just like it was with rattlesnakes, the rules were that you pinned your opponent down for the count of ten and then you raised yourself high into the air -- the sign of victory! The snakes know what their bite can do to another snake of the same kind, but they refuse to use this deadly force. Maybe we can call this the snakes' code of ethics.

If so, then the snakes (and these two men) are more disciplined than many of us who call ourselves civilized human beings. In 2016, there were roughly 17,250 murders and homicides in the U.S. For a country that many view as a "Christian Nation," the brutality of Americans against Americans is very high. Yet, we claim to be civilized.

So what does it mean to be civilized? A civilized person is one who is polite and courteous and does not take advantage of someone who is vulnerable and weak. A civilized person respects the boundaries of others and does not intrude into their lives uninvited. Civilized people do not have to kill or destroy one another, because all problems and issues can be resolved without violence. Civilized people seek to do the right thing, regardless if it benefits them or not.

Jesus had a few things to say about how civilized people ought to live. Love one another as I love you! Have compassion with your fellow human being! Go the second mile with those who are in need. Provide an environment of true friendship with all people. Do not let your pride and selfishness get in your way of doing the right thing. Do unto others as you would have others to do unto you.

So to say that someone is mean as a snake is really an insult to the snake. Snakes seem to do it better! They refuse to use deadly force on their own species, which is higher ground than a lot of our fellow human beings subscribe to as a way of dealing with personal conflict. There are a lot of people in this world who need to rise to a higher ethic, so as to become as good as a snake.

Where are you on this scale?

NEED A LIGHT?

In his book, *Lord of the Rings,* Tolkien uses the concept of light and darkness to bring meaning to the life of his characters. The darker the situation and the degree of distortion of the characters portray the depth of evil that has embraced these unfortunate creatures. The more hideous the creature, the less human they have become. Darkness equals evil!

Tolkien is on track with the biblical use of light and darkness. In the beginning, God said, "Let there be light and it was so." This bit of information was not written to inform us how light came into the universe, but that God has the ability to bring light into the darkness of our world. God is Light and his Light can overcome any darkness in our world and within us.

Jesus proclaimed to his people, "You are the Light of the world." Or we might hear: "I have overcome the darkness within you. Do not be afraid, my Light is with you and within you. In the darkest night and the dreariest of days, my Light will be upon you and remain within you.

In the Gospel According to John, Jesus proclaims that all God has given to him he has bestowed upon them. We are at all times being embraced by the One who continually overcomes the darkness that would consume us. To discover God is to discover self! We come from God and in Him we find our meaning for life and our purpose for living. The cloud is lifted and we now see the pathway before us.

John Bunyan in his classic book, *Pilgrim's Progress*, paints a picture of the Christian journey as being filled with uncertainty. There are various traps along the pathway to be avoided at all costs. The struggles and hardships are part of the territory. The important question to ask here is not why we have to endure such pain and suffering, but what will we do with it. How will we allow it to transform our life?

In The Beginning God brought forth his Light and it overcame the Darkness. This Light that was in the Beginning is in you. The song goes; "This little light of mine, I'm going to let it shine. Let it shine! Let it shine!" "Embrace the Light that embraces you, live as Children of the Light." Ephesians 5: 8 (*KVJ*)

I am currently reading Victor Hugo's book, *Les Miserables*. The main character, Jean Valjean (Zhan-Val-zhan), has put his prison time behind him and with the help of Bishop Myriel found new life. He is now mayor of a small town east of Paris. He owns and operates a factory, which has become the source of income for most of the community. He helps the poor and the outcast. Even to those who despise him, he shows compassion and willingness to help them in times of trouble. He has become a most valuable resource for the community, but he has broken the provisions of his parole by moving to this community. Lucky for him, another man is identified as being Valjean. The man is arrested and put on trial with the possibility of going to prison. It is an easy out for Valjean. All he has to do is say nothing. He could rationalize that without him the factory would die a slow death. The poor and outcast would not get the help they desperately need. There were a thousand and one reasons why Valjean should be quiet and say nothing, but that's not what he did.

We are told that he listened to his conscience, which told him it would be wrong to say nothing. When Valjean stepped forward and identified himself as the true Valjean, he allowed the Light within him to surface and flow upon all around him.

We will always have a thousand and one reasons why we should not do what our conscience keeps telling us to do. This voice within us, which seeks to guide us in the ways we should go, is often the voice of God. It comes forth from the *Imago Dei* (Image of God) that resides within us. The scriptures tell us that God is Light and within Him there is no darkness.

Are the lights on in your life?

NEED HELP

It seems that a certain hiker in the mountains of Western North Carolina wasn't looking where he was going and fell over a cliff. Luckily, he was able to grab hold of a bush growing from the side of the cliff. Dangling from midair, he began to cry out: "Help! Is anybody up there?"

To this reply came the response: "Yes, this is the Lord, what do you need?"

The hiker replied, "I need you to get me out of this situation. What do you want me to do?"

To this the Lord replied, "Just let go."

For a few moments there was silence from the side of the cliff, and then a voice could be heard: "Help, is anybody else up there?"

Often it is in the difficult situations that a new perspective is discovered. That is, the negative experience of life brings enlightenment to the positive side of life. Death ennobles life. Darkness praises the light. Hunger kisses the pieces of bread. Sickness teaches the meaning of health. These are lessons we would rather not experience, but for the most part the decision is not ours to make. Christianity teaches us that life is born out of death, and the meaning of life is often found in suffering. Hope is found at the foot of a Cross.

The Preacher in the Old Testament, more popularly known as the Book of Ecclesiastes, tells us that there is a season for everything under the sun. Every season has something very special to offer life. Whether it is the "worst of times or the best of times," there is a unique meaning hidden below the outward appearance of things. Remember that not all things are what they appear to be.

It is easy just to stay in our comfort zone and enjoy life from that perspective. The down side to this is our learning curve hardly moves at all. Since we are not challenged in our understanding of self, God, or our world view, we make very few adjustments to our lives. The disruptions of life can rock our boat, take the wind out of our sails, bring a sense of fear, uncertainty, and doubt that forces us to make some adjustments to return to a feeling of homeostasis.

The Preacher reminds us that there is a time for everything. There is a time to build up and a time to tear down, a time laugh and a time to cry. It is this variety that challenges us to make needed changes in life.

God has placed Himself right in the midst of life where people live and die. Therefore, those who suffer may do one of two things:

❖ Hide behind it, that is, become bitter over it and give up on life all together, or

❖ Offer it back to God and allow Him to use it for His glory. It then becomes our gift to God.

I suppose the events of last year have given our nation and the world much to think about in this area and I can only imagine that this year will present us with many more opportunities. May God grant unto us the courage to live our lives in the direction of the future possibilities!

Need help?

OLD REPORT CARDS

Recently, as I was going through a box of old papers that my mom had saved from my school days, I came across all of my report cards from the 1st grade through the 12th grade. It was a real eye-opener for me. As I looked through one report card after another, I realized that I was very fortunate to have graduated. My grades made it apparent that I either did not know how to study or did not care to study or maybe both. I failed the third grade and was moved up to the next class because of all the baby boomers coming into the school system. There was nowhere to put me, so I got a break!

In my defense, I was hyperactive and had an attention problem. There are medications available today for kids with that condition, but not in the 50s. Still, somehow, someway I got through it all and eventually graduated from high school. A number of my friends were planning to enroll in the new Spartanburg Technical College, which was due to open in the fall of 1963. I had no other plans at the time, so I took an entrance exam to determine what educational course would be best for me. Con-sidering my high school record, I knew that this was going to be a washout. I wouldn't fit in anywhere. But surprise, surprise my scores indicated that I could take any course being offered.

So I asked, "What courses are you offering?" As in the movie "The Graduate," when Ben had a conversation with a family friend about his future and heard that plastics was the way to go, the director of the school told me that electronics was the way to go, so I said ok.

It was a tough two years of school, but I made it through and got my Associate of Science Degree in electronic technology. At that time a number of my friends were going into the Air Force. Since that was the branch of service I liked best, I decided that was the way for me. Again I took a test to determine what I was best qualified to do. I had no idea as to what that might be or even if I would score high enough to get into the Air Force. I got a call in a few days, and the recruiter told me I had a perfect score on the electronics portion of the test. Holy cow, I didn't think that I had learned much of anything in electronics school, but something must have stuck with me.

The next thing I knew I was off to the military induction center in Charlotte, NC. I wasn't sure I would pass the physical. I had had rheumatic fever three times: at age seven, age eleven and the year I graduated from high school. I had been diagnosed with a heart murmur, which meant one of the heart values was not closing properly. At the end of this day filled with various tests and a lot of other things I won't mention, I was summoned to come forward and get my results. I expected the worst, but to my surprise the gentleman said, "Welcome to the United States Air Force, Mr. Ford."

I was totally surprised!   "You mean I passed everything, sir?"

His response was: "With flying colors! You will take your oath of office in the room behind me in 30 minutes. Don't be late!"

Two hours later, I was on a plane to Lackland Air Force Base in San Antonio, TX, for basic training. After eight weeks I went to Biloxi, MS, and electronic school. The goal was to become a navigational specialist.   I had learned more than I thought at Spartanburg TEC, so the school at Keesler AFB was not that difficult.

With nearly a year's study of general electronics and various navigational systems under my belt, I was shipped off to Charleston AFB and then soon after that to Alconbury AFB in England.   Next I was back stateside, first at McConnell AFB in Wichita, KS, then to Homestead AFB near Miami, FL and finally to George AFB in California.

My training had served me well. I had worked on the navigational systems on C-124s, C-130s, and C-141s, as well as, F-105s and RF-4Cs. My skills were on the flight line, which is where we determined which black box had gone bad. There were enough black boxes on any given plane to keep you busy for months, if you kept pulling the wrong one to take to the shop for repairs. You needed to be right the first time to have the plane back in service and ready to fly. I was very good at making the right selection.

Since all the evaluations I received were at the highest level, just a little over three years into my tour of duty I was promoted to Staff Sergeant. What more could I ask for? My skills and hard work had paid off. You would think I would have developed some confi-dence in my ability to study and learn new things, but that was not the case.

Returning home after my tour of duty, I got a job with Western Electric as an installer, which I hated and eventually quit. Next I got a job with WSPA-TV in Spartanburg, SC, as an engineer at the transmitter site high atop Hogback Mountain near Tryon, N.C. It was then that God began His work of calling me into ministry.

I had felt this call before, but just ignored it, thinking that it would go away. It had for a while, but now it was back. Finally, one day, I made God a promise. If I could get into college (still didn't think my high school performance would make that possible), I would give it a try.

So on a Saturday morning I found myself at a gram-mar school on South Church Street in Spartanburg. I was taking the SAT. Maybe after this God would leave me alone and I could go back to Hogback Mountain.

My scores were sent to Spartanburg Methodist College, about five miles from my home. When I received a letter from Spartanburg Methodist College, my first thought was that it was nice of them to send me a letter letting me know that I had not been accepted. I didn't want to see it, so I had my mom to open it and read it. I can still remember her voice when she said to me, "Well, Bob, congratulations, you are now a freshman at Spartanburg Methodist College."

I couldn't believe it. God had pulled a fast one on me. This was not supposed to happen. The letter was supposed to have read, "We are sorry to inform you that you have not been accepted into Spartanburg Methodist College." I was not prepared for a letter of acceptance.

Things from the past have a way of haunting us. We think we have put it behind us, and then it pops up again. There was always a good crutch for me when I was afraid to try something new. I could just say to myself, "Well, you know Robert, you're not that smart. You shouldn't go getting into water that's too deep. You don't have the right stuff. You will only fail." Lucky for me, God has always placed people around me who saw straight through my flimsy excuses and challenged me to discover my true potential.

It has been important for me to have people around me who believe I am capable of doing some great work for the Lord. After about 50 years of various roles in ministry, I must say that I have been surprised by God over and over again. I did not realize He could do so much with so little. It has been an amazing journey. I have been truly blessed in so many ways that I can't begin to count.

Every time I meet a character in the Bible who is reluctant to follow God into the unknown, I am reminded of myself. So many were wrong, from Jeremiah the Prophet who thought he was too young, to Moses who thought his speech impediment was too much to overcome, and Mary Magdalene who thought her bad marriages and her bad past as a prostitute would disqualify her. God overcame the bad past and produced some quit astonishing results. As you remember, Mary Magdalene was last to leave the Cross and the first at the Tomb. She was the first person to proclaim the Gospel.

So, got something in your past you need to let go of?

ON THE ROAD TO FINGERVILLE

It was early afternoon on that Saturday when Donald Greenway knocked on our door. He came to tell me his father needed a ride up to Fingerville, just north of Spartanburg, SC, and a good place to go if you wanted to buy some moonshine. Mr. Greenway, a small, slender man, who at the time was probably in his early 50s, was a weekend drunk. He worked at the local textile mill and remained sober during the week, but when the weekend came, he had to have his liquor.

In South Carolina at the time, you could get your driver's license at the age of 14. I had just received mine a few months before, and I was willing to drive Mr. Greenway to his desired location.

Off we went in Mr. Greenway's '54 Buick on the Yellow Brick Road to Fingerville. Mr. Greenway was by my side in the front seat with his son Donald by the door. In the back seat were Freddie Greenway and two other kids from the neighborhood.

As we traveled down some back roads, Mr. Greenway felt we were not going fast enough, so he put his foot on mine and mashed down. The old Buick responded, and soon we were now doing about 60 or 65 mph down a road I had never been on before. As we descended a hill and approached a curve, I was horrified to see a one lane bridge up ahead, with another car approaching from the other side. It was too late to stop our car, so the only other option was to cross the bridge.

I do believe that Mr. Greenway was already a few sheets to the wind – as in, drunk-- that day. I aimed the car as best I could, fully expecting to meet the other car at some point on the bridge, but it never happened. Somehow two rather large automobiles crossed on a one-lane country bridge at the same time. How this happened, I did not know. Even today, I feel as though it took a few years off my life. Interestingly, Mr. Greenway, entered the bridge drunk and exited sober.

We continued our trip to Fingerville and to the house where Mr. Greenway insisted he could find the best moonshine in the area. On the return trip, he never interfered with my driving. We had skimmed the edge of death and lived. God had performed a miracle on that bridge, and we all were allowed to go on living.

Facing death the way we did left its mark on some of us, while others simply thought of it as a lot of good luck. For me, it brought an awareness of God into my life. I knew that we had not survived because of my good driving. God was with us and we knew it not. God had saved us, and we took it as good luck.

Was there any lasting change for any of us who had traveled so close to death that day? I'm afraid not! We should have pulled over to the side of the road, gotten out of the car, bowed down toward the bridge and offered our thanks and praise to the living, active God who is always among us. We should have offered our lives up to God and surrendered to his will and destiny for each of us, but we did not.

What does it take for God to get our attention? I mean our undivided attention, which puts us alone with Him. What does it take for us to **"be still, and hear the voice of God?"** The work and activity of God in any event of life is not obvious to the eyes and ears. It is easy to miss and hard to find. Why should it be this way? Should it not be that God is hard to miss and easy to find!

Think about it, at the birth of the Christ Child, only the family was present. Some years later, on a Cross outside the city gates of Jerusalem He died with two thieves, one on His left and one on His right. In the face of death, one experienced the presence of God; the other did not. What was the difference? Did God love one more than the other? The famous passage of scripture from the Gospel According to John says that **"God so loved the world, that he provided a historical person to walk among us and suffer with us and for us that we might have life and have life in abundance."** (*Paraphrase by RLF*)

Therefore, the problem is with us, not God. The mandate from the scriptures is that **"if we seek, we will find."**

What will it take for God to get your attention?

OUT OF OUR COMFORT ZONE

There was once a small village located near the shore-line of some very treacherous waters. Throughout the year many ships would run aground and needed help in getting the passengers to safety. Despite a local lighthouse's warning ships not to get too close, many charged on into the rocks that protruded from the swirling waters.

So the small village organized a rescue squad to go out in their boats when a ship was in trouble, to rescue the folks in danger. It was a lifesaver. As the years went by, the small rescue hut was transformed into a modern building with all the comforts of home. So comfortable, in fact, that when a call for help was sounded no one wanted to go out in the cold winter night into a restless sea. Somewhere along the way, the folks at the rescue station had forgotten why they were there.

It is possible to grow comfortable with life to the point that we develop a reluctance to make any changes. It is often said of those of us who refuse to make any changes that we live so close to the forest that we can't see the trees. In other words we live too close to ourselves to have an objective view. We may be oblivious to what might be obvious to others.

During my post-seminary training, I became a part of a CPE Group (Clinical Pastoral Education). My CPE supervisor was The Reverend Doctor John Edgerton. He was sharp as a tack. Like a skilled surgeon, he would cut deep into our inner souls to reveal something about us we did not know or maybe we did not want to know.

There is a scripture that says that the truth will set us free. In numerous accounts of Jesus' life, He set individuals free from their inner fears, faults, and failures that had been kept hidden deep in the inner self. From the woman at the well to the tax collector Zacchaeus, Jesus performed His surgical procedures.

I have sat through more worship services than I can count. Coming out of the evangelical tradition, I am accustomed to the ending invitation to come and surrender to the call of Jesus Christ. I am also aware of how difficult it is for most people to do that. The bottom line is that we have a fear of discovery and acknowledgment of parts of our lives that we don't want to deal with. It is a call to come out of our comfort zone and to face up to our need of God in our lives. It is the fear of the life that we would be called to live and the fear that we might not be able to live up to the high standard of life we are being asked to embrace.

One of my favorite passages of scripture is found in The Gospel According to Matthew, where we have the words of Jesus addressing the crowd around him:

> Come unto me all you that are heavy laden and I will give you rest. Take the yoke that I have made especially for you and you will find rest unto your souls. You will find life more uplifting and invigorating and meaningful in your relationship with me.

It has been my experience that what Christ has called me to do in life, He has always equipped me to perform. Over and over again in my life, He has surprised me with how He can do so much with so little. I'm not the brightest star in the sky, nor am I the most eloquent speaker known to mankind, but in spite of all the imperfections I could list about myself, He has accomplished some pretty amazing things with me.

I could not have done any of it if I had decided to stay in my comfort zone. It would have been easy to remain in my cocoon, but I choose to take the risk of coming out into a world full of possibilities for me and that has made my life worth the living.

Are you willing to leave your comfort zone?

PEA RIDGE ADVENTURE

It was the summer I went to Polk County, NC, to visit my first cousin, Roger Fowler. Roger was an outdoors kind of person, so at some point during our time together we would go down to the river and spend the night in a tent with a group of guys. Fishing was part of our activities for the late afternoon. Roger was good at catching fish and not a bad cook. For him, it didn't get any better than catching fish and cooking them over an open fire along with some sort of beans. And just in case the fish were not biting, he brought along some other items of food.

Being out under the stars at night did give you a feeling of freedom and being at peace. Although I was considered a city-slicker, I seemed to fit in rather well with the other guys. It felt like I had been a part of the group all my life. The main topics of discussion were hunting trips, fishing techniques, and girls. The first two topics were out of my expertise, but the girl topic was more to my liking. At some point in the late evening hours, the fire would die down and sleep would fall upon our small band of adventurers.

When our alarm clock went off the next morning, that is, when the sun came up, it was time for breakfast, which consisted of eggs and bacon, kept fresh in the ice cooler overnight. After breakfast, it was the norm to take a dip into the cool, refreshing river flowing by the campsite. Oh yes, our bathing suits were the kind that you were born with, so we were all in fashion. I think the proper term here is "skinny dipping."

On Saturday afternoon, Roger and I would thumb (also called "hitchhiking") into Tryon to see a movie. It was about a 30-mile trip each way, so we had to leave a little early to ensure we would get there on time. It was not as much of a problem getting to Tryon as it was getting back. The movie would be over by 9:00 or 9:30 in the evening, so it was beginning to get dark .

Not to waste time, we would start walking toward home in hopes that somebody would come by and pick us up. On this particular night, we were in for a real treat. A car stopped for us a few miles down the road from Tryon. We got in the back seat, and off we went. Two young men in their mid-twenties were in the front seat having a conversation that did not include us. As we sped along at about 75 to 80 miles an hour, the driver asked us to give him another beer from the cooler. I quickly found the cooler and the beer. This kind of beer can did not have a pull tab to open it; you needed a "church key," as it is so often called. So using the church key, I opened the can of beer and handed it to the driver. I remind you that we were still traveling along at a high rate of speed, and it bothered me when the driver took his eyes off the road to look back and see how I was doing in getting the beer. Speed was the essence!

Sometimes we were on our side of the road, and sometimes we were on the other side of the road, but still on the road. When we started out, we were in hopes that the trip home would not take too long, but we didn't have this in mind. With tires squalling as we went around curve after curve, I was hoping that the driver would not ask for another beer. Eventually we came to a road that led to wherever they were going, so they let us out.

Boy, it felt good to be back on solid ground. The ride had been more exciting than the movie we saw. But as dangerous as the ride had been, we had made it without a scratch. You can bet that we kept this experience to ourselves, because this kind of information in certain hands might endanger our chances of doing this again.

From the point of departure from the car, we had about a three-mile walk, which was quite enjoyable. Walking under the stars on a clear night, out in the open country with no lights, except for the moon that was in full glow, we just felt so good to be alive. The stars were visible all over the place. Every now and then a passing car would interrupt the silence of the night. It was the kind of experience you don't get in the city, which was well worth the trip.

During my junior and high school years, I made an annual trip back to Pea Ridge and the opportunity to experience life at a different pace. The wide open country and the majestic mountains of western North Carolina provide an excellent opportunity to relax and experience life from a different angle. In the late afternoon you can see the clouds slowly making their way over the mountain tops and from there to the valley below. It is hard to forget the beautiful display of colors as the sun makes its descent and hides itself behind the Blue Ridge Mountains. The eventual darkness has such a peaceful feel about it. A front porch rocking chair is the perfect place to experience this amazing show of God's wonder.

Here are the words of the psalmist as he reflects on the glory of God's creation.

> O Lord our Lord, how excellent is your name in all the earth! You have set your glory above the heavens. . . .When I consider your heavens, the work of your fingers, the moon and the stars, which you have put in place, in all of this I wonder, what is mankind, that you would give any thought to them? You even take the time to visit all your children, wherever they may be. You have made mankind a little lower than your messengers, and you have bestowed upon mankind the crowning point of your creation. You have given to mankind the responsibility of taking care of your creation and having power to influence it... .O Lord our Lord, how excellent is your name in all the earth! Psalm 8 (*Paraphrase by RLF*)

On one of the trips to the moon, one of the astronauts took a beautiful picture of the earth. You would never know from this picture that there were any living creatures on earth. If you could take a picture from the sun, you would be lucky to find the earth. The universe is huge! There is more to it than we will ever know. Yet, in all its vastness, God has zeroed in on the population of our world. God has given an enormous amount of time and effort to this species called *homo sapiens*.

We are special in God's eyes. We are made in the *Imago Dei* (Latin meaning Image of God). Like nothing else that we know of in the entire universe, we are offered special communion with God. God's spirit dwells with us and abides with us in all of life's situations. The New Testament states that God sent his Divine Mediator to guide us to our Creator. The Jesus of history is our Divine Mediator, and connects us with our Creator God.

The Good News is that no matter how small or insignificant you may consider yourself to be, God knows where you are and who you are. In all of life, you are embraced by God. You are in the eyes of God as valuable as any other human being on the face of this place we call earth. In the quiet of the night, be still and hear God's spirit speak to you.

Do you have eyes to see?

Ears to hear?

RED, RED WINE

It was a Friday night and there was not a lot going on at Farley Ave. Ext. near Spartanburg, SC, so I decided to go up to the local café/convenience store to get a hotdog. The store didn't look like much from the outside, but they made some of the best hotdogs in town. It so happens that a few of my friends were there and at some point we got on the subject of wine. Ed Wilson, the Fonze of our group, suggested that we walk up to another café about half a mile away, which sold a variety of alcoholic beverages.

On the way there, somehow I stuck my foot in my mouth by saying that wine did not have much punch to it. Of course, this observation was coming from the mouth of a 14-year-old, who did not know what wine tasted like. Ed, who was probably in his early twenties, said that he would buy all the wine I would drink. It sounded like a good enough offer to me, so I took him up on it.

The wine of the day was called "Seven Star," which was probably the cheapest wine on the face of God's green earth. I don't know how much I drank, but on the way back home it began to hit. My ability to walk and talk was deeply impaired, but somehow the guys got me back to my house. They sat me down in a rocking chair in our front room and turned on the TV set. It would have helped if they had pointed me in the right direction, but at this point, I don't guess it mattered.

My dad worked the third shift at Saxon Mill, so not long after being placed in my living room, I heard him getting up to get ready for work. I decided just to stay put and play it cool. Eventually, he came into the room, took one look at me and said, "Son, you'd better go to bed!"

My response was something like, "Ok Dad, I think you're right!"

As I tried to make my way from the living room to my bedroom, I had to pass through two other rooms. I thought if I could make it through the door that led into the kitchen, I would have it made. I made that transition ok, but noticed that a TV tray lay in my way. This was the kind of tray that was on a stand and stood about 3 feet off the floor. Thinking that I had performed the right maneuver, I caught one of the legs with my foot and over I went. Oops, there goes another TV tray! I finally made it to my bedroom, got into bed, forgot about taking my clothes off, and turned out the light. Ah, safe and sound!

Mom worked the second shift at Spartanburg General Hospital as an LPN. She would usually get home around 11:30, just before Dad headed off. On this particular night, as they passed in the living room, Dad said something like: "I think your son is drunk. I sent him to bed, so you might want to check on him."

I lay quietly in bed, thinking that nothing would be said. That ignorance was soon put aside when all of a sudden my bedroom light came on and Mom began to yell at me, "What have you done?" At the same time, she pulled my covers off me, reached down, grabbed me by my shoulders and began to shake me like a container of salt.

I'm telling you, this sort of treatment will always get your attention. To the best of my knowledge, I told her what had happened that night. I promised not to do it again and assured her I was sorry that I had disappointed her. There's a certain bond between a mother and her son, especially if the son is an only child. So, her temper was short-lived, which was to my advantage.

Although there were never any alcoholic beverages in the house, I had seen my father drunk on a number of occasions. Dad and his drinking buddy, Paul Ford, would often go out on the town over the weekend. While Paul cleaned up his act and put the wild life behind him, I don't believe my father was able to do that. So from a very early age I considered drinking a part of life. Smoking and drinking were two bad habits I learned by watching my father. As the saying goes, the apple didn't fall too far from the tree.

I'd like to say that was the last time I ever got drunk, but it was not. It happened on many occasions while I was in the Air Force. I suppose that if I were going to become an alcoholic it would have happened then. Those days, at an Airman's Club you could usually get any drink for $.20 cents. When I was stationed at McConnell AFB in Wichita, Kansas, every Friday the Air Force would bring pizza and beer to our workplace, as we all celebrated the arrival of the weekend. I don't know whose idea this was, but it was a big hit with our navigation unit.

I am thankful that when I was discharged from the Air Force and came back home, I made my way back to church. It was there that I began to receive some spiritual healing. The minister at my church gave me a book called *The Confessions of Saint Augustine*. Augustine lived a wild and crazy life. He admits that if it had not been for the prayers of his mother, he would never have made it back from his trip to the far country. He also stated that the most difficult thing he had ever done in his life was to discover who he was. He discovered that to know our true selves is to know something about how God works in our lives. He went on to become one of the most influential Christian writers of all time.

In spite of Augustine's misdirected life, God got him on the right track and did some great things with him.

What mistakes do you need to overcome?

SCHOOL BUSES AND KIDS

It was an opportunity of a lifetime and I was not about to pass it up. All 10th graders who wanted to get their school bus license could sign up for the three-day class. This was back in the days when all our school bus drivers were high school students in the 11th and 12th grades. I passed the written test and the road test, which meant that I would soon receive my license in the mail.

While my grades were not good enough for me to be a regular school bus driver, I was allowed to fill-in on an as-needed basis. The opportunity to fill in for one of the regular bus drivers came quite often. The students on the bus informed me of the route I was to take. I'll have to say that most of the time they were honest with me.

At railroad crossings, I would select the biggest boy on the bus to run the tracks, which involved leaving the bus cross the tracks to see whether or not a train was coming, and then wave as a signal when the coast was clear. I would pick the track runner up on the other side of the tracks. I don't think this procedure is used anymore, but in those days, it seemed to work just fine.

One of my stops was at a grammar school, which included first to sixth grades. Boy, talking about a group of noisy, rowdy kids! This group had them all. On a few occasions I had to pull the bus over to the side of the road and give them a lecture. It was a simple message and to the point: "If you don't sit down and be quiet, your parents will be taking you to and from school for the remainder of the school year." Things would settle down for a while, and then the next day we would be back at square one.

Even as an 11th and 12th grader, I knew their lives were in my hands, and I took full responsibility for that. It did not make me the most popular bus driver at school, but at least I tried to run a tight ship or, in this case, a tight bus. I protected the weak from the bullies and the innocent from the guilty. I had the power to ban any kid from using the bus, and I used this power to insure that all were treated fairly.

The school bus I usually ended up driving was the one with the difficult gear shift. All the buses were manual shift, so you had to go from first gear to second gear to third gear and fourth gear and finally fifth gear. That's how it was supposed to work, but hardly ever that easy. The gears had a habit of hanging up if you did not shift in a certain way. I hated that part of driving a school bus.

Making turns down some of the dirt roads I had to travel were a challenge. The roads were narrow and had deep gullies on both sides. Not much room for error! In spite of the noise, gears, and the roads, I made my rounds without incident. I would then take the bus back to the school parking lot for buses and leave the keys in it. The regular driver would pick it up sometime later on in the afternoon.

Over the years, school buses have all gone to automatic transmission, and perhaps bigger and better motors, but the cargo remains the same: children that depend on a safe trip to and from school. Jesus knew the importance of children. While He was making His rounds on foot, some children attempted to come to Him, but the adults were preventing them from doing so. Jesus intervened, welcomed the children and used this incident as an opportunity to teach His disciples about the Kingdom of God.

> Truly I say to you, unless you are converted and become like children, you will not enter the kingdom of heaven. Whoever then humbles himself as a child, that person is the greatest in the Kingdom of Heaven. Whoever receives one such child in My name, receives Me. But whoever causes one of these little ones who believe in Me to stumble, it would be better for that person to have a heavy millstone hung around his or her neck, and to be thrown into the deep sea. Matthew 18: 3-6 (*Paraphrase by RLF*)

What is it about children that we adults ought to imitate? The question that preceded this discussion of children came from one of the disciples who wanted to know who would be greatest in the Kingdom of

Heaven. Jesus responded that it would be people who humble themselves. The next passage of scripture speaks of stumbling blocks in the world, and points out that there is a price to pay if you are the one causing stumbling blocks to be formed.

A newborn baby must be nurtured by someone in order to live. Small children do not know what they need, are unaware of the dangers around them, and have no way of caring for themselves when they are sick. Even as they grow into adulthood, good parents still check up on them to see if they are ok.

During the time I served as chaplain in a local hospital, I visited a 94-year-old female patient, who in spite of her own healthcare needs was worried about her 74-year-old daughter, who was going through some difficult times. She was not willing to let go of her parental responsibilities.

Jesus saw all humanity as the children of God. We, as a children of God, we must accept our vulnerability and need for God's guidance and protection. This is what we are asked to bring with us in worship and life. Our goal is not to become self-sufficient, but dependent upon our Heavenly Father, our Heavenly Mother. As Jesus said so poignantly, "O' Jerusalem, Jerusalem, how many times I would have gathered you to myself as a hen gathers her chicks under her wings, but you would not?" (*Paraphrase by RLF*)

Whose wings are you under?

SEINING FOR MINNOWS

It was a hot summer day in the Grace Cotton Mill Village, located just outside Rutherfordton, NC. Not a lot was going on. Normally there would be a baseball game in the large pasture just down the road from my home, but not today. Racing bicycles was a popular sport among the kids in the village, but no bicycles were in sight today. Even the watermelon man who always came by on Saturdays was nowhere to be seen. Gosh, what is an eight-year-old kid to do under such conditions?

Well, I guess I could go down to Mr. and Mrs. Johnson's grocery store and get a Nehi Peach Dope for one nickel. Just a little background info at this point! For some reason all drinks were called "dopes." I don't know if this came from some of the early drinks such as Coca Cola and Pepsi Cola having had some form of cocaine in them or not, but around our neighborhood that's what they were called. I don't know how many times one of my parents would tell me to go to the store and get a carton of dopes. Well, on this hot summer day I decided that I needed a dope, so off I went to Johnson's Store.

In the store, I ran into James Reece, a classmate from Ruth Elementary School, and he was about as bored as I was. His uncle had gone fishing during the week and had caught a lot of fish, so James thought it might be a good thing for us to do. Not far down into the woods behind my home was a small creek, which usually had a number of minnows swimming around. So we each went home and borrowed a pillowcase from the closet and off we went to seine for minnows. Up and down the small creek we went trying to convince these small creatures that they needed to go into our pillowcases. I can't remember if any of the minnows took us up on our offer, but we had a great time trying.

When you're out having fun like this it seems that time passes very quickly. Before we knew it, evening approached, and we heard a voice from the distance. I was surprised that it was not the voice of my mother. Instead it was James' mother letting him know that if he failed to come home right away he was going to get a whipping.

So we did the only sensible thing to do: James ran toward his house and I ran toward mine! My mom was not looking for me yet, so I was safe and sound. But not so for James! He got the whipping of his life. While I hated that, I was glad that it happened to James and not me. Well, you never know, James and I might have been destined to become great fishermen, but not on that Saturday afternoon. In fact, I think the whole thing kinda turned me off about this thing called "fishing." I think James was a little upset with me that I didn't get a whipping like he did, but I was an only child and usually we only children could get away with more than the kids that had brothers and sisters. At least this was true for me!

In the Gospel According to Mark, we are told that Jesus was just casually walking along the shoreline when he came upon two fishermen named Simeon and Andrew. Jesus said to them, "Come follow me," and immediately they dropped their nets, jumped out of their fishing boat and did as He bid them. A little further down the shoreline, Jesus came upon two more fishermen, this time named James and John. When Jesus invited them, they immediately responded as Simeon and Andrew had.

I wonder how that went over in their homes when they told their wives:

> Hey honey, I just sold our boat and fishing gear and for the next two or three years I'm going to be living with a group of men. As our schedule permits, I'll drop by from time to time to check on you and the kids. I'd like to talk to you more about it, but I've got to go now. Bye.

As Paul Harvey would say, "That's the other side of the story never told." As you know, scriptures never give us the full panoramic picture of life. We get only a thin slice of the experience of the individuals who are introduced to us. Life at home for them seems not to be of interest to the biblical writers, but it is a subject not to be overlooked. It would have been highly unusual for a Jewish boy not to have been married at some point in his early teens. You have to remember that their life expectancy was in the mid- to late-twenties.

With those kind of odds you don't have a lot of time to mess around; you need to get on with the process of family and children. Large families were the norm because the mortality rate for children was so high. So to ensure that you had someone to carry on your name you would have a lot of children. Yet in the midst of this urgent need of family and children, comes another urgent call. "Come Follow Me!"

It becomes a real life dilemma! What is a person to do? The fact is that the call of God always creates a dilemma for the individual being addressed. The "Come Follow Me" is a summons to drop what you are doing or plan to do and follow the direction of the call. It is a call to action, not waiting. This is the point Mark was trying to convey to his audience. James and I, too, heard an urgent call we could not ignore making its way through the woods. We both threw down our seining nets and ran for home. It was the right thing to do and we knew it.

The call "Come Follow Me" is the call to come home to God.

Whose call are you heeding?

SURPRISED BY GOD

We had met on my trip to this small Western North Carolina community. I was a member of the Gardner-Webb College "God Squad," known as FOCUS (Fellowship Of Christians United in Service). We came into town with our Bibles, youth activity notebooks, and sheet music for the leading contemporary songs. We had more energy and enthusiasm than knowledge about what we were trying to do — revitalize the youth program at Longview Baptist Church.

Because of my work schedule, I was unable to join the team on the first day of our three-day event. So on a late Saturday afternoon I wandered in a direction that led to this quaint community. It was early evening and darkness had settled as I desperately attempted to find my destination. After several trips up and down the same road, trying to find a building with a steeple on it, I finally settled on the place where the most cars were parked. But still not quite sure that this was the place, I drove around in the parking lot looking for any signs indicating that this was Longview Baptist Church. Fortunately, through the glass windows I saw one of the team members behind the pulpit. Yes, this was the place. I waited outside the sanctuary until the service was finished. After the closing prayer, as I made my way into the sanctuary, I caught sight of a young lady making her way to the front. Her long reddish brown hair and short dress had caught my eye.

The evening was just beginning as our team made our way over to the pastor's home for fun and games with the youth. Team members training to be ministers of education and youth, took the lead. I took a seat out of their way and became a spectator. As a single ministerial student, I was always on the lookout for some young lady to be my co-pilot in my journey into the ministerial vocation.

As luck — or should I say, "the hand of God" — would have it, I ended up in the home of Wayne and Juanita Newton, the parents of the sprightly young lady I had noticed at the church. The student minister of music and I were guests in their home, staying in the downstairs area. This strategic location gave me the opportunity to get to know Wayne and Juanita, as well as their daughter, Gail. Before the weekend was over, I found a way to get the Newtons to invite me back for a future visit. As I recall that was my only other visit to the Newton home before I graduated and was off to New England to do some work for the Home Mission Board of the Southern Baptist Convention.

After that came seminary in San Francisco. I had not planned to go home for Christmas, because of the expense of flying. Mom and Dad had other ideas, so with their help I made it happen. During those two weeks, I managed to get in a visit or two with the Newtons in Longview, where I discovered just how much Teresa Gail Newton meant to me. I don't know if it was love at first sight, but I was sure she was someone I wanted to get to know better. As I drove away to return to San Francisco, I knew I would be finding my way east. On my return to the campus of Golden Gate Theological Seminary, I started making plans to transfer to Southeastern Theological Seminary, in the town of Wake Forest, just twenty miles north of Raleigh, NC.

There is a saying that a man chases a woman until she catches him. Such was the case for me. On one particular evening when we were out on the town, Gail held her hand up to let the lights shine on a ring she was wearing. Playing the part of the village idiot, I asked, "What's that ring on your finger?"

Softly, but clearly, she said: "Oh, it's my grand-mother's engagement ring."

The next thing I knew we were at a jewelry store buying a ring. Before I knew it, we were engaged. Now as we look back over our nearly 42 years of marriage, we both realize our meeting was no accident; it had the hand of God written all over it. In the first place, I was not a member of that FOCUS Team going to Longview. Jackie Millwood was on the team, but he also was scheduled to sing with a quartet. He could not be in two places at the same time, so he asked me if I could go to Longview in his place. The rest is history. I never knew that going to Longview would be a life-changing experience for me. Neither did a young lady by the name of Teresa Gail Newton or her parents realize just how the weekend was going to impact them. It was a

God thing. We were all very surprised by what lay in store for us and the blessings that God poured out on us.

God breaks into the routine activities of life and makes known to us His will, His purpose and His destiny for us. We very seldom know when it's coming, but when it does, we are never the same again.

We modern humans live and work in the mundane world of Chronos Time. Kairos Time is God's time. While you don't set your clock to this time frame, you will know it has broken into your Chronos Time. When it happens, things change. What you do with or about that change is up to you. You may try to ignore it, or oppose it, or receive it. "God's up to something, and you are invited to participate in the moment." It will change your life.

Are you ready to be "Surprised by God?"

THE BIRTH OF A CHILD

It was a cold winter's day and some snow was beginning to accumulate on the ground. Inside the home of Manley and Bessie Ford a child was trying to come into the world, but with some difficulty. The mother-to-be was a small-framed person, weighing probably not much more than a 120 pounds. It was her first attempt at motherhood, and it would be her last. The struggle went on for hours, as Dr. Gold waited with the family for nature to take its course. In a back room of the house, Emma Lou Skipper Ford lay struggling to bring this child into the world. It was a struggle that would go on through the night. There was no pain medication, just words of encouragement from family members eagerly waiting.

Just a month before, another baby had come into the world on that same bed. Lilian Ford Ellenburg had given birth to her daughter, Evelyn. Seems this place had become a birthing center. In fact two other babies had been born here: Harold and Joyce Ellenburg. So this child would be the fourth to be born in this room and on this bed. The only question that remained was WHEN? At 3:00 am on December 19, a six-pound baby decided to make his appearance much to the relief of his mom! He was given the name of Robert Loran Ford.

Nearly twelve years later, at Frye Hospital in Hickory, NC, another six-pound baby was born to Wayne and Juanita Newton and given the name Teresa Gail Newton. Her grandfather stated that he was going to call her Gail, after his favorite TV personality Gale Storm.

In that same hospital, decades later, Robert would be watching as his wife, Gail Newton Ford, struggled to bring their child into the world. Never mind that it took all night. Finally, at 9:20 am on November 17, Lauran Gayle Ford decided to come into the world. Weighing? Six pounds, of course.

I have been reminded on several occasions that I know nothing about bringing a baby into the world. I have to admit that I didn't experience the same kind of pain my wife did. In fact, it made her mad while she struggled to give birth that the hospital brought me breakfast. Believe me, after a night of watching her suffer through all of this, I was plenty hungry. I was her coach, so I needed lots of energy to do my job. It went something like this, "Now dear, breathe in and breathe out. Just relax and everything will be ok." Somehow these words did not bring a great deal of comfort to her, and she let me know in a very stern way. I was walking on thin ice, and I knew it.

The struggle of birth is a prelude to the struggle of life. Growing up is not easy and helping a child through the process of growing up is a great challenge. The story of the pregnancy of Mary and the eventual birth of her son, Jesus, is from start to finish a tale of mystery and intrigue. Again we lack details about the actual birthing process, but Matthew and Luke make it perfectly clear that the life of this child would be contested from beginning to end.

The ingredients of faith, hope, and love are vital factors in a long-term relationship. Without these factors, you just have people living together for mutual convenience. The bottom line is that developing and maintaining relationships is a process of give and take. Sometimes one person in a family gets all the attention. This is not healthy. In other families one person gets all the blame if something goes wrong. This, too, is not heathy. From the wisdom of Proverbs we have these thoughts: "Parents take responsibility for training your child in the ways that are true, good, and wholesome and that child will be less likely to deviate from it; or if he or she does fall away, will mostly likely to return to their good upbringing." (*Paraphrase by RLF*)

A child was born, a child is born, a child will be born. A family formed.

What ingredients can you provide?

THE CALL OF DUTY

I was just fresh out of the Air Force Electronic School at Kessler Air Force Base in Biloxi, MI, and on my way to Charleston, SC, Air Force Base. This would be my first permanent assignment, and I was looking forward to putting all my training to work. Charleston Air Force Base was part of a Military Airlift Command. As a navigation specialist, I worked on the various systems on C-124s (affectionately called "The Shaky"), C-141s, and the work horse C-130s. Going into the cockpit of a C-124 was like climbing up a three-story wall. That was the highest cockpit I'd ever seen. I am afraid of heights, but the call of duty trumped my fears, and each day the trip got a little easier.

Just three months later, I received orders sending me to Alconbury Air Force Base near the small community of Huntington in England. Alconbury was part of a Technical Air Command. RF-4Cs ruled the day and could not fly unless the Inertia Navigational System (INS) was working. The INS was unique in that it did not send out any radar signals to determine its navigational path, which meant the enemy could not easily detect this plane. The RF-4C contained the FLR and SLR systems, which allowed the pilot to film the countryside below roughly about 120 miles across.

One morning, my squadron of RF-4Cs was assigned to take the lead in a joint training operation with the British Royal Air Force (RAF) Fighter Jets. Although I was not scheduled to come in until 7:00 am that morning, at 4:00 am I was out on the flight-line making sure our INS Systems were ready for the challenge. All our planes passed the pre-flight test except one, but that one plane could give our squadron a "black eye." I reported this to the crew chief, who, in turn, passed the information on to Command Headquarters. Another plane was substituted and all went off like clockwork. I had saved the day!

At times we need to go beyond what is required of us. Jesus spoke of this as recorded in the Gospel according to Matthew: "Whoever (this more likely would be a Roman soldier who would demand that you carry his armor for him) compels you to go one mile, go with him two miles." In life, we often have to do tasks we really don't want to do. When this demand comes from our work place or from one of our family members, it can be difficult to refuse to do what has been asked of us.

One day Peter came to Jesus and asked, "Lord how many times shall I forgive someone who sins against me?"

The answer he received was: "Up to seven times seventy!"

While the number "7" signifies perfection in Jewish theology, Jesus responded that he should forgive a person as many times as the person needs forgiveness. Defined that way, forgiveness becomes a little more difficult to muster.

So what does this mean for everyday living? As was true with the Roman soldiers of Jesus' day, at any moment constraints may be added to our lives. While all of these acts are not abusive, they often make us feel as though a great burden has been put on our shoulders. These acts of extra duty that interrupt our plans may create a lot of ill feelings for us. This is why Jesus addressed the issue. Over time one could accumulate a lot of negative energy. Negative energy is a burden to the soul.

One day as Jesus spoke to a rather large group of people, he invited those who were carrying great burdens to bring them to Him. "Come unto me," He said, "and I will give you rest. . . .

> Take the yoke I have for you. It has been made especially for you and it will fit you perfectly. It will allow you to find rest for your troubled soul. You will begin to live life to its fullest. Your energy will return and you will find great joy walking with God through life.

Can you go the second mile?

THE COMMODE

My mother had just received a phone call from one of
our relatives. It seems that my cousin Randy had come
down with a deadly disease. It was called "spinal
meningitis." Our family did not know if he would live
or die. For a ten-year-old like me, this was earth-
shaking news. How could someone so young be in
danger of dying? Later in the day I went into the
bathroom and made my way to the commode. I closed
the lid, knelt down, placed both elbows on the lid and
brought both hands together in a praying manner. I
can remember bowing my head and asking God to
help my cousin live.

A week or so later, we were informed that my cousin
was going to make it. Whatever treatment was being
administered was helping him get over the disease.
We were all so very happy for Randy. For me, I
wondered if my prayer at the commode had anything
to do with Randy's recovery. For some reason, I kept
it all to myself.

I suppose it doesn't matter as much where we pray as
it does that we pray. Daniel prayed in a lion's den.
Paul prayed in a jail cell. Jesus prayed from a cross.

Driving to and from work, my wife offers up her prayers to God. So, I guess you could say that on occasions, a commode may be a good place to start.

In his book, *Healing Words*, Larry Dossey, M.D., writes there are so many forms of prayer that it is almost impossible to find one definition that fits all. Prayer, as taken from the Latin word "precarius," means to obtain by begging and the word "precari" which means to entreat, to ask or to implore. We can petition God for something for ourselves or we may offer a prayer of intercession for the needs of others. Confession of our sins is a form of prayer. Also, we may offer a prayer of thanksgiving for what God has provided.

Prayers may be expressed with words, signs, or silence. The postures people take in offering prayer are as numerous as the prayers themselves. Eyes may be open or eyes may be closed, it doesn't matter. The head may be lifted up or bowed. Hands together or hands up lifted, it's all the same. Praying can be done alone or in a group.

Another way in which our prayers may be expressed is through our dreams. Unfortunately, we often remember very little of our dreams, so it is hard to determine what our deeper, inner soul is speaking on our behalf. When we are asked if we pray, our response of, "Not as much as I should," simply refers to our conscious prayers, and not to the unspoken ones. Dossey refers to Ann and Barry Ulanov, who state in their study of prayer that it is a phenomenon that starts and ends without words. Perhaps the Psalmist was onto a good thing when he wrote: "Don't say a word, and listen for God to speak; be still and become aware of His movement around you and through you." Psalm 46: 11 (*Paraphrase by RLF*)

In a more practical sense, our day-to-day life speaks volumes to God concerning our needs, so with this in mind, it may be impossible not to pray. Essentially, prayer emanates not only from our words, but from our lives. Perhaps the loudest prayers are the prayers that are unspoken.

Our prayers lead us into the mystery of God. We are looking for answers, which seem to never come our way. Why is this happening to me, to someone I love? We will soon discover that prayer is not about answers, but our willingness to stand within the mystery of God without answers. It has been stated by Gertrude Stein that the answer is there is no answer.

It has been suggested by the German poet, Rainer Maria Rilke, that sickness is the process by which the body rids itself of the bad stuff. In sickness there is a waiting period, this is the standing in the mystery of God. It is a time to be still, to wait, and wonder what it is that God is doing with us. It is the time of the greatest opportunity for spiritual growth and enlightenment. If you miss this, you miss the deeper meaning of the sickness. All sickness leads toward a spiritual direction, one we may not know! It seeks to chart a new course in our journey through this world and to lead us into parts of our inner being that may be foreign to us. Hold on, close your eyes, there is a lot more to come. Like a roller-coaster ride in the dark!

Prayer is not so much about bringing God into our lives, as it is about bringing us into God's life. God is always where He needs to be. God is always doing what He needs to do. It may be difficult to understand that illness is as much a perfecting event as anything else that may happen to us. In fact, there is a theory that both health and illness co-exist in each one of us. One will dominate for a while then the other.

The words of Jesus in the Garden of Gethsemane, "Not my will, but Thy will be done," form an appropriate approach to God for us to use in our prayers.

The goal of prayer is not to bring God into our lives. He's already here. Our goal is to enter into God's life.

Have you made that move yet?

THE ELDER SON

After studying Rembrandt's painting of "The Return of the Prodigal Son," Henri Nouwen says that the elder son, located to the right and in the foreground, appears to be withdrawn. He looks at the father, but not with eyes of joy. He does not reach out, nor does he smile or express welcome. He is just standing there, unattached.

The father and his lost son dominate the left side of the painting, while the elder son dominates the right. Nouwen also makes note of the space between the father and the elder son, which perhaps expresses the mental, emotional, and spiritual separation between them.

Nouwen wonders what the elder son will do? Will he just walk away without saying anything to his father or his lost brother? He does not appear to be ready to embrace his brother as his father has done. There is a similarity in the dress of the father and the elder son, which conveys a sense of power and strength. Both experience a light that is shining across their faces, but the similarity ends there. The light upon the father flows through him into his hands, which embrace the lost son. The hands of the elder son are folded and covered by the darkness.

To Nouwen, this depicts a parable of *two* lost sons. The elder son is lost in his obedience. He lives his life to please his father and thereby receive his father's blessings. He is committed to doing the right thing. He walks a narrow line and worries that he may have veered off the path to the left or to the right. His life has no gray within it; it is all black and white. No room for foolishness or fun. He is jealous of his carefree brother, who dares to break all the rules and then has the nerve to return home asking for forgiveness. "He made his bed, now let him sleep in it" is the attitude of the elder son. "This brother of mine will receive no forgiveness from me."

As Gene Rollins says in his book, *Behind the Masks*, the elder son has lived into the mask he wears proudly to the point that he has become the mask. This is a very unhealthy condition, because his mask prevents him from knowing who he really is. What he doesn't realize is that he, too, is lost, as much as his brother. Just in a different way!

If you recall the story, you will remember all of the family and friends are invited to come to a banquet and rejoice in the return of the son who was lost, but now is found. Everyone will be there except the elder son, who is full of envy. He cannot let go of the plow. He cannot allow himself to enjoy the benefits of his hard work and dedication. The banquet is the father's offer of Communion. By refusing to participate, the elder son shows that he, too, needs to be embraced by the father, but will not allow that to happen. This reminds me of the words of Jesus when he said:

> Jerusalem! Jerusalem! How many times I would have gathered you to myself; as a hen gathers her chicks under her wings, but you would not.

The elder son is, of course, correct that his brother has no right to this reception. What he fails to see is that neither does he deserve being invited to the banquet. He has lived as though he has "earned" what he has received from his father, and that any gifts are yet somewhere out there in the future, not a present reality. Maybe in light of this, we are more like the elder son than the younger son. We keep acting as though the fullness of our Father's gifts to us are still in the future. We'll get them when we get to Heaven.

Over and over again, Jesus informed his disciples that the "Kingdom of God had come upon them." Not just a portion of the "Kingdom," but the full "Kingdom" has been poured out and given to all of God's children, which includes every human being on the face of the earth. Home (Heaven) is not some far, far away place up there. It is among us. It surrounds us. It embraces us. It is within us in the present moment.

Who are you, the younger or elder son?

Which one reflects the life you have lived?

What are some of the things that keep you away from the father's embrace?

What mask are you currently wearing?

THE EYES OF GOD

Lord, you have looked me over up and down. You know my inner thoughts, feelings, and desires. Lord, there is not a place in the world I can go to that you are not there. Even if I try escaping you, you will find me.

For some reason, you are determined to be a part of my life. You are persistent, Lord, and not willing to give up the chase. But I'm afraid to be caught, so I will continually try to get away from you.

For some reason, you brought me into being. From the very beginning, you knew what you wanted to do with me, but I struggle to know what I want to do with You. I should know the answer to this question, but it escapes me.

I try to hide the wickedness within me, but I know it is there. I need for you to overcome it and free me from my captivity. Surely, there is no one else who can help me. What I hate in others, I continually find in me.

Lord, continue to look me over up and down. As you allow me to discover you in all aspects of my life, may I also discover more of who I am in light of how you see me. For this reason Lord there is hope for me and all who, like me, struggle with the demons within and those that surround me.

To know me is to encounter me and to bestow upon me all I need to know you and to know me. I am not forgotten. I have not been left behind. Hope abounds around me. Renewal is at work in my life.

Help me to see what you see Lord, and to accept that as the real me. Thank you Lord for not giving up on me, even in the darkest of times, and for leading me away from death to life! (*Paraphrase by RLF*)

Over the years of my life I have been done in by a lot of people who told me they could help me with my problem or problems. I discovered that they did not want to help me, but to use me for their own purpose. It is disheartening to experience betrayal from someone you thought wanted to help you, especially if you considered that person a friend. I have loaned money never to get it back. I have paid a lot of money for services that were never provided and the money never returned. I get aggravated with myself for being such a fool. Why can't I learn who the good guys and the bad guys are in life?

Here's the deal with me, if you don't already know it by now. I am a trusting person. I want to help a stranger or friend who seeks help from me. If I have something that I think you need, I'll give to you. That's just me! I believe that most people want to do the right thing and will treat you fairly if you treat them fairly. I know, I know the old saying that a sucker is born every minute. Yes, one of those suckers is me.

My pain has taken a variety of directions. I have been hurt financially, physically, mentally and emotionally in my journey through life. It was as though I had on my head a sign that read: "I'm gullible. Take advantage of me." A variety of emotions have surfaced in my life as a result. I have found myself deep into anger and frustration. I have thoughts of taking revenge. My wife says I'm passive/aggressive! Maybe I am! I realize that no one makes me angry, sad, or happy. All that stuff comes from within me, specifically that part of me I don't like to deal with. Most of the time I keep it all deep within my soul, but there does come a time when I cuss and fuss and sometimes scream and holler just to rid myself of these horrible feelings. Of course, I do all of this in private and not in the presence of others.

Beyond what I do in private, here's what I do to deal with it. I become a clown. Not literally, but figuratively! I hide behind by sense of humor. All of us comedians are hiding from something; we just don't want the rest of the world to know about it. So, I just pretend to be ok like everybody else. I don't want to be thought of being different. I like being like everyone else, although I don't usually feel like everyone else.

I say that, but in truth I don't want become like the people who hurt, disappoint and take advantage of others (including me). I want to be me: a trusting soul who cares about people and animals! Some years ago, I was sure I had hit a dog on a country road. I stopped to take care of it, but couldn't find it anywhere. I enlisted the help of friends, and returned to the scene again. No dog. Apparently the dog was fine, but I was a basket case. Do I wish I could have just walked away? Of course not. That's who I am.

The God we meet in Psalms 139, who knows us and everything about us, will never take advantage of us! I can always be me and know that I am in good hands, or should I say, the best hands. In spite of all of my issues, weakness, and vulnerabilities, God always does for me whatever is in my best interest, because He sees the worst, but also the possibilities in me.

Whose eyes do you trust?

THE FIRST PITCH

The challenge for supremacy was on the line. It was a winner take all. They stood there looking at one another for a long while. Who would go first? Finally the opposing team captain stepped forward and took from his playbook a cantation that was sure to work. With his best melodious voice, he sent forth a chant that was sure to reach into the high heavens and beyond. Once he finished, he stepped back and waited for the desired results. As he stood there with the rest of his team, all with greatest expectations, he soon acknowledged that nothing was going to happen. So, he stepped forward again and from another page of his playbook he choose a very reliable chant that from ages and ages ago had proven to work in very difficult situations. The results were the same: nothing happened. Desperation set in, so a barrage of chants filled the airways and still nothing happened.

Then a little scrawny man stepped forward from the opposing team. He looked as though a good puff of wind would blow him away, but this was all deceptive. Hidden beneath all this outward display of humanity was a powerful force.

One day a prophet was running for his life. It was a time when religion and politics were brothers and sisters. You could not have one without the other. Because there was a bounty for this prophet, no one would help him lest they, too, might be added to the most-wanted list. So what could he do? Where could he go? He found a cave. Totally alone, he did not dare move or make a sound. Feeling all alone and abandoned by his friends and family, he entertained the thought of suicide. His life had become of no value or purpose. Without hope that things could get any better, he curled up in a fetal position and waited for death to consume his body.

Outside the cave there was a fierce storm, followed by an earthquake and then an intense fire with great intensity. At last there came a Stillness more powerful than the wind, rain, thunder, lightning, earthquake or fire. Out of the Silence, God stepped forward. Out of the Silence God spoke. Out of the Stillness God created.

Having discovered God in his stillness and silence, the prophet now was raised from his self-imposed tomb. The old man had passed away. A new man came forth from the cave, a man with a mission. His people needed to feel and experience the transforming power of God. They, too, needed to be delivered from their tombs of spiritual death. Like the Lone Ranger riding into town and saving the day, the prophet was equipped and ready to take on that role.

It is no coincident that as the Jesus of History hung from the cross, there came a deep darkness upon the face of the earth and from the deep darkness came an earthquake that shook the world to its foundation. . .then thunder. . .then lightning. And finally a stillness that filled the earth. This was no local event; it was felt throughout the universe. If we are so inclined to believe, it was the Second Big Bang.

The Book of Revelation speaks of the Third Big Bang in the Second Coming of the Christ of Faith. Again, this will have universal implications. In the final analysis, God will have the last Word. It is through and by this Word that the old things will pass away and the newness of God will come forth.

The prophet's words are echoed in the voices of the disciples of the Christ of Faith. As the Apostle Paul puts it, "We are new creatures in Christ." We who have experienced the Stillness and Silence of God through the Divine Mediator are the living promise of this coming reality of God. He offers us this Stillness and Silence as expressed in The Gospel according to Matthew:

> Come unto me, all you that labor with life and are heavy laden, for I will give you rest (peace). Take the yoke I have made especially for you. It fits you to a tee. When you do, you will learn an important lesson about me. You will learn that I am meek (not over powering) and that I am a humble soul (lowly in heart). Then you will experience the rest I have for you. You will be at peace with yourself, your fellow human beings, and most importantly, you will be at peace with God." Matthew 11:28 (*Paraphrase by RLF*)

Our mission, if we accept it, will be to become channels of God's creative process, knowing that this process is more powerful in our silence! Jesus often withdrew from the world in order to re-engage the world. This is the ebb and flow of life, bringing balance to us and to those we seek to touch.

Are you willing to accept your mission from God?

THE FIRST SERMON

I was tired of running. The chase had exhausted me and no matter which way I turned, there he was pursuing me like the hound of heaven from Francis Thompson's epic poem. I had gone to the far country, seeking some escape from his glaring eyes, but that did not work. Finally, I made my way back home in the hope that I would be left alone, but that did not happen. Bit by bit he drew me in like a fish that has struggled for so long and then in total exhaustion finally gives up. There was no need to resist anymore. No need to hide! I had been found and there was nothing to do now. I was ready to take my punishment.

It was a Sunday morning. I can't remember the exact date, but I was determined to end this thing once and for all, so I got up from my seat and made my move. Slowly but surely I made my way down what seemed to me to be a long and endless aisle. Finally, I reached my destination in emotional shambles. I could not hold back the tears that began flowing down my cheeks. I was a nervous wreck. Then a hand and next an arm reached out and embraced me. Since I was unable to speak, he spoke for me.

I agreed to follow God's call for me. It was a vocation I would not in a million years have chosen, but God had some bright idea that it was right for me. So believing that He could make no mistakes, I finally said yes, but with one stipulation, I had to have some training. If I could not get into college the deal was off. Just plain and simple! My grades through grammar school and high school were barely passing. In fact, I had failed the 3rd grade and nearly failed the 7th grade. I knew that odds were against me. I figured a snowstorm in July was more likely than my getting into college.

Soon I was taking the SAT. Since I didn't even know there were books that prepared people to take this test, I went into the valley of the shadow of death totally oblivious. A week or so later I got my score (1130), and Spartanburg Methodist Collage accepted me. I had made it over the second hurdle, but I was in shock. How in the world did I do that?

Then came a turn of events that rocked my world! The Reverend Buddy Moore, my pastor, had to be away for a Sunday and asked me to fill in for him. Had this man lost his mind or what? I knew so very little about the Bible and even less about how to present a sermon. He insisted, so I put together twelve pages of notes. (I have no memory today of what I wrote.)

All week I prayed for a blizzard to come so that the service would be cancelled. Once it appeared that was not going to happen, I began praying that we would have a very small crowd that morning. On a normal

Sunday morning around 130 people attended our worship service. On my Sunday, there were more than 200. Boy! What about that the scripture that says: "Ask and it shall be given?" As I looked out over the crowd that morning, I experienced a great deal of fear and trembling—like I had read about in the Bible.

When it was time for me to step up to the pulpit and say something that would make sense, I realized I had twelve pages of notes for a thirty-minute sermon! Again my emotions got the best of me as I tried to speak. Ken Watson, the minister of music, came forward, put his arm around me and whispered, "Bob you can do it. God is with you."

So off I went into my delivery, and in about twelve minutes I was through. I had missed my goal by nearly 18 minutes. In the Baptist tradition, an invitational hymn follows the sermon, and to my surprise there was a movement from the congregation that I could hardly believe. People were lined up on all three aisles, coming forward to make some decision concerning their relationship with God.

Since then, I have given a good bit thought to this response, and I have concluded that it was God's way of saying to me, "See what I can do with your life if you will follow me." The bottom line is that we should not underestimate what God can do with our lives if we are willing to trust Him with the results. The outpouring of God's spirit that morning upon me and the congregation produced the result He desired. I have been amazed over and over again by God's ability to use me in ways I never dreamed could happen.

One of my favorite songs is "It Is NO Secret." I especially love the line that says: "What he has done for others, he will do for you."

Are you willing to step forward and see what God can accomplish with your life?

THE HANDY MAN

Jerry was a handyman with a big heart. A mild manner and soft voice characterized his demeanor. His work was always the very best it could be, because he was so particular about the end results. At my home, he fixed water leaks on the roof and in the garage, each done to perfection.

Only some time later did I learn of Jerry's willingness to share his home and resources with those less fortunate. There a lots of examples, but two I know about he essentially made part of his family. A young homeless woman facing the world with a couple of children to raise and no family to help her through his help was able to get back on her feet, land a job and find a place to live and raise her family. A young man going through difficult times found there was a place for him and a purpose he had yet to discover, when Jerry hired him to help with the handy man jobs that were popping up all over the place.

You don't meet very many people like Jerry who have such a huge heart and capacity to let go of their lives in order to help others. I regret that I did not meet him sooner. I would have been willing to become one of his disciples, sitting at his feet and gleaming from him the true meaning of why we are all on God's green earth. Very few people knew of his capacity to give to others in need, mainly because he never made a big deal about it. He simply did the best job possible and charged a fair price for his work. You always got what you paid for with Jerry.

Jesus told his disciples that if they wanted to find life, they needed to give it away. On the other hand, if they decided to keep their lives for themselves, they would lose out. His promise was that it was more blessed to give than to receive.

Getting can become an addiction, like all addictions not easily overcome. Our society is perhaps the most materialistic one in the world. This I believe is evidenced by the number of "yard sales" that occur across our land. The primary reason for "yard sales" is that we have collected too much stuff and we need to get rid of it so we can buy more stuff. Why sell it when we can give it away to someone or an organization that deals with folks who are down on their luck?

There is a saying that goes like this: "Do all the good you can for as long as you can and you will find a fulfilled life with purpose and meaning." This was how Jerry lived his life. When he died, his adopted families were included in his last will and testament. Jerry, as the saying goes, put his money where his mouth was.

Do you have what it takes to become God's Handy Man or Woman?

THE LONE MOHEGAN
IN THE BOAT

The call that comes at some point in life was looking me square in the face! What would I do with this persistent call that would not leave me alone? To no avail, I had travelled halfway around the world trying to escape. Sometimes when we are running away from something, we need to stop, turn around and face it head on.

I am reminded of Jacob's encounter with an Angel of the Lord at the River Jabbok. They wrestled until the break of day, leaving Jacob with a displaced hip and numerous scrapes and bruises. At the end of this wild encounter, the Angel of the Lord gave Jacob a new name. He would no longer be known as Jacob, which in Hebrew carries the meaning of "cheater," but now would be known as Israel, which carries the meaning in Hebrew of "God contends." The name change was an indication that a major change had occurred in the life of Jacob.

This would be his calling and the destiny for him and for his family. The calling that had confronted his father and grandfather was now given over to him. It is an awesome experience when God lays hands upon you and says: "I have called you to take my yoke upon you and to bear my burden that I have for you into a world that will not readily receive you or respond to you."

In fact, you will feel like you are the only Mohegan in the boat. Like Jacob, having wrestled with the Lord for quite some time, I went away limping, but with a new calling and destiny for my life. Since training precedes the call to action, I applied for entrance at Spartanburg Methodist College, an exciting place to be. I soon discovered there were no other ministerial students on campus. Boy, talk about feeling like the Lone Ranger.

Having completed my first two years, I was off to Gardner-Webb College, in beautiful downtown Boiling Springs, NC. With classes starting on Monday, the college offered an outdoor vesper service. While I had just finished a week of instruction in sermon preparation and delivery offered through the campus chaplain's office, I still felt like a loner. Since I was in my mid-twenties at the time, I attributed my isolation to the fact that I was older than the other students I had met. The price you pay for getting a late start.

In fact, I had chosen not to stay on campus, because the dorms seemed to noisy and congested. As an only child, I had to have my space. Mrs. Hamrick rented three upstairs rooms in her home in Lattimore, ten miles up the road from the college, to ministerial students and only to ministerial students. I had one room and another student by the name of Jerry Burleson had one room, which meant that there was one more room for rent. I had no idea who my upstairs

128

roommates would be, but they had to be a lot less intrusive than the group on campus.

As I made my way back to my car that Sunday evening from the vesper service, I heard a person walking near me say, "Hey! I'm Dennis Hester, a new ministerial student on campus."

"I'm Robert Ford, and I'm a ministerial student too."

That simple encounter made all the difference in the world to me. I had found a "bird of a feather." I was not the only Mohegan in the boat. When Dennis said the conditions for studying were not good where he was staying, I told him I would talk to Mrs. Hamrick about his needing a good place to stay. It worked! Within the week Dennis had the third bedroom.

Maybe Dennis and I had both felt like we were the only Mohegan in the boat, but after that Sunday evening, we put that all to rest. We graduated from GWC and eventually ended up at the same seminary. Our friendship has lasted over the years as we have shared our struggles and failures, as well as our many stories that describe how God took two unsuspecting souls on a journey that no one would have thought possible.

We are never alone in a boat, for there is always that mystery guest that rides with us.

Are you ready to come on board?

THE MAN ON A HILL

I stood there looking down at my cousins, just daring one of them to try and pull me off the high bank I'd perched myself on. For that moment in time, I was King of the Hill, a title and place everyone wanted. I had the advantage and they knew it. But as fate would have it, I slipped and fell. My few minutes of fame were gone, and now I lay at the bottom of the hill, angry with myself for being so clumsy.

Our game of King of the Hill would go on it seemed for hours with laughter and a few bumps and bruises, which had a short life span. It was a game, only a game and we knew that it was not for real, but we enjoyed each other's company. I was close to all of these cousins. We were family, and that made all the difference in the world.

We are all grown up now, and we have neither the time nor the energy to play King of the Hill. But what we have not put aside are our ties that bind our hearts, minds, and souls with a lasting appreciation for one another. While getting dirty is not high on our list of things to do, being in the company of one another is a most cherished experience. We still laugh about days gone by and sometimes at each other, but never with the desire to hurt, bend, or mutilate.

This is what family and the stranger in our midst ought to look and feel like. A healthy family can facilitate the healing of its members. Embraces (both physical and emotional), along with hugs and kisses, affirm we are wanted, accepted, and loved. Touch is more powerful than speech. Touch involves being aware of who we are and fully connected to the place and the people who surround us. We touch with our eyes as we listen actively. We allow the hurt and pain they feel to radiate into our inner souls. Their pain becomes our pain and our resource for healing.

It had been a hectic week for the sojourner and his family. They faced the big city that awaited them with mixed emotions and expectations. He would soon become the King of the Hill, but unlike the childhood game, here no one wanted to take his place. One by one the crowd moved away from him. Soon his family would be gone as they scattered here and there throughout the city. The pain was too much for them. They could not bear it or acknowledge it.

On the lonely hillside, there he was; placed between two death row inmates. His whole body ached. The nails that had pierced his skin made their marks, which would become a permanent tattoo on each hand and each foot. It was his pain, but it was more than that: it was his exposure to all hurt and pain that radiated from all mankind. In return, his healing filled the earth. Again the miracle of God's creative was at work in and through his servant to bestow healing upon all of humanity. Pain becomes healing, and healing is painful.

So there he stood, arms outstretched toward the east and the west, and against his back a vertical pole pointing down toward hell and up toward heaven, as is often believed. There is nothing that can separate him from his family. He will bring them into the fold. No one will be left out unless they choose to be. But he is not one to give up so easily.

The King of the Hill summons us to come and partake of his goodness. To drink his wine and eat his bread! He will not step down, for he has been lifted up and seeks to lift us up. He is true to his promise, "If I be lifted up, I will draw all of humanity to myself, that where I Am, you shall be also. I will not leave you or forsake you."

Are you willing to take your place with him?

THE MOTHERHOOD OF GOD

The story of Creation is the story of the Pregnancy of God. All that is came forth out of God, and God looked upon His newborn Creation and declared it to be good. The child called Creation was perfect as perfect can get.

Within this new birth there existed another pregnancy that we will call "The Garden of Eden." Like the womb of a mother-to-be, the Garden had all the needed ingredients for the growth and development of each and every fetus within it. As we know, a delivery day comes when it is time to leave the protective environment of the womb.

If you were to take away the apple episode from Adam and Eve, they still would have eventually left the Garden behind to go and discover all that God had created. There is a simple principle here: we must leave home in order to discover who we are and our purpose in life. We cannot live in our mother's womb forever, and neither could Adam and Eve live forever in the womb of God.

In the second account of Creation, found in Genesis 2:23, that woman was taken from man and she became

133

his partner in life. The scripture then states in verse 24, "That is why a man leaves his father and mother and is united with his wife, and they become one." The process of becoming one occurs when they each discover themselves in the other person. Not only has the wife been taken from the husband, so likewise the meaning of the husband's life will only be taken from his wife. Therefore, they both hold a special place in the life of the other. What one does to the other, he or she does to the self. To destroy the other is to destroy the self, because the two are one. To find themselves in the other, they must both leave home, which has been their womb.

At birth the umbilical cord is cut, separating the child from its mother. At the wedding, the umbilical cord (figuratively speaking) is cut again. The minister or priest announces that the two have become one. The only question to be answered is which one do they become? The ongoing creative power of God unites the two, and the minister or priest announces that, "What God has brought together, let no one put asunder." The couple has within their relationship the creative power of God at work bringing some-thing new into the world.

This act of leaving home to find home is repeated over and over again in the biblical accounts. Jacob is forced to leave home (similar to the birth process) and eventually finds himself. His brother finds himself when he leaves home to make amends with Jacob. There in an open field, they embrace and forgive one another. Again, it is in the face of the other that they find meaning for their lives. They go their separate ways, but take a bit of each other with them. They both are at peace with themselves and with God. Life is good!

In the New Testament, the same is true for the Prodigal Son. He leaves home, goes to the far country and experiments with life while discovering the downside of being disconnected from those who give meaning to his life. He goes away from home and finds himself in order to go home and be connected with family, which has the potential for empowering him to make more discoveries of self.

Dorothy is picked up by a whirlwind (similar to the one that Ezekiel experienced) and transported to a strange land. In this forbidden place, with help from three friends she discovers the true value of life. She will return home a new person. Of course, we come back home to reconnect in order to leave home and continue the journey of finding ourselves.

The New Testament presents the process of being "Born Again." This is placed in the context of a spiritual awakening. The Prodigal Son experiences a spiritual awakening when his father embraces him. Being born again is the process of discovery of God in our lives and our life in God. This is the continuation of God's creative process in each and every life. No one is left out! No one is overlooked! No one is forgotten! All the earth and human kind are the result of God's birthing process. This is to say that God is both Father and Mother of all things created. In this process, the Motherhood of God should not take a backseat in our theology. As the husband and wife are equal, so are the Motherhood and Fatherhood of God.

A good book I suggest you read is *The Shack* by William P. Young. The Motherhood of God is prominent in this story of finding healing in the midst of a great loss. The read will be well worth your time.

Can you allow God to mother you?

THE POWER TO BLESS

Once upon a time there were two brothers who were quite different in their talents and abilities. One had a cattle and dairy farm, while the other grew some of the best-looking vegetables you ever laid your eyes on. The father, a lover of good T-bone steaks, was partial to his son who fed his appetite. Over a period of time, it became evident to the other son that his contribution to the family was not appreciated as much as his brother's. He felt some detachment and aloneness and longed for his parent's blessing, which seemed to always elude him.

A prominent theme throughout the Old Testament is the blessing of the father. The Good Housekeeping Seal of Approval was extremely desirable and sought after by the sons. Sorry girls, it was a male-dominated society, as it still is today, but we hope getting better. The son receiving the blessing was assured of success and would receive the larger portion of the inheritance. Again, this was no small matter, and as with Cain and Abel, Esau and Jacob, Joseph with his coat of many colors and his eleven brothers, and the disciples of Jesus, it became a matter of contention.

The blessing of the parents on their children is an important part of the developmental stages of life. It is the bestowing of acceptance and affirmation on the life of the child. It conveys a sense of self-value and importance and also impacts the child's world view, which may go something like this: "I am a person of value and I have a lot to give to the world in which I live"; or "I do not have a lot to offer my world, so I will get what I need the best way I can."

Even in the New Testament, Jesus was not impartial with his disciples. He does not take all of the disciples with him on the trip up the Mount of Transfiguration. He takes with him Peter, James, and John. These men are the top three and continually receive the blessing of Jesus that is not offered to the other disciples. In the Gospel according to Mark, James and John come to Jesus asking for one to sit on his right and the other on his left in his glory. They were asking for a special blessing and a special place in his kingdom.

To be left out of the blessing of our parents, our boss at work, or our pastor at church leaves a void in the life of those who so desperately seek and need the affirmation. After a while you discover that no matter how hard you try, you will not receive the blessing that you seek.
The division between siblings is a common factor in many families. The perception of not being loved by a parent or parents is a heavy burden to carry.

Parents need to know that they have this power to bless, and it ought to be used intentionally to ensure that all members of the family feel special. Certainly there are special needs children, and the other siblings should understand this and accept it for what it is. In general, though, the rule goes like this: the child who best conforms to the parents' wishes is the one who receives the blessing over and over again. The other children are told that they need to be like their brother or sister who is the high achiever. The problem here is their feeling they are put on the face of this earth to become like someone else. Instead, we are here to discover who we are by discovering our abilities to be creative with the tools of life that have been given to us.

This does not mean that being different is bad or wrong. Actually it may mean that one child is gifted in another area and is comfortable living outside the lines or boundaries the parents have imposed upon the children. That is, you should be this way or that way and if you're not, then you are not up to par with the rest of the family and you will not receive the blessing you desire.

My father started working in a cotton mill when he was 14 years old. At some point in time he decided that I was not going to work in a cotton mill when I grew up. As an adult, I learned that the mill had a summer program for the millhands' children. We could work at the cotton mill as a summer job and perhaps we, too, would choose textiles for a vocation. My father never told me about this program. He did not want me to follow in his footsteps.

In some cases, a mother or father will have the expectation that a daughter or son should take over the family business or choose the vocation of one of the parents. Again the power to bless is at play in this scenario! I have this belief that we are created with certain potential. We are given certain gifts and talents to use in our pursuit of a meaningful life. We may describe our gifts and talents as the calling of God. That is, we have these gifts and talents because we are unique in the eyes of God. We are like snowflakes: no two are exactly alike.

The challenge of life is to discover our uniqueness, embrace it and cultivate it. Putting it the Army way, we all should seek to be the best we can be. Barbara Streisand sings that people who need people are the most fortunate people in the world. We all need help from others in the discovery of our value, purpose and meaning in life.

A gift discovered is a destiny placed before us. With it we have the power to bless and to be blessed.

Can you accept this challenge?

THE STRANGER IN OUR MIDST

Excitement among the village people was at a high pitch! On this day they would be in the presence of the most talked about man in the country. It seems that everywhere he went good things happened! So the whole village waited in anticipation of what he might do for them. Eventually he showed up with his entourage and positioned himself in the center of the great crowd gathered around him.

His first words were a mystery to everyone:

> In my presence, the Kingdom of Heaven has come upon you. I am the gateway by which you may enter into this Kingdom. Among all the pathways to God, my pathway is supreme. In fact I am the one and only way to the God you seek. I want you to know that there is a place for all of you. No one is left out due to some restrictions by the Kingdom. With me you will discover the Kingdom that is within you and surrounds you.

During his time with the people he used terms such as the Kingdom of God, the Kingdom of Heaven, and the Reign of God to describe the family of God.

He did not talk to the people about their membership with a local congregation and how to become a member of some religious organization. But he also did not discourage such affiliations. His teachings pointed to the context of God in the marketplace. This is where one just might be confronted with a Kingdom issue.

It is in the mundane world of survival that God takes His daily walk. There was a time that He took walks in a garden, but now He stood before them looking like a normal human being, but unknown to the crowd He had brought the Kingdom of God near to them. He presented a Kingdom not about exclusion, but inclusion. His message was not about how to keep people out, but how to bring them in. This Kingdom was big enough and open enough for all people. He never brought up how a person ought to be baptized or what they should wear before God. This was not what the Kingdom was about. The Kingdom transcended the physical world and directed the people toward the spiritual world. God is spirit and those who would commune with Him must do so via the Spiritual Presence of God.

There is a popular view that the United States is a Christian nation. This is a false view of Christianity and the Nation of God. The word "nation" or "*ethnos*" does not refer to a particular nation in the world, but to all persons, groups, or institutions whose spirituality reflects the image of God into the world. Therefore, membership in a local congregation in itself does not constitute evidence that members of that organization are living in the Reign of God.

Matthew says that all kinds of people not considered part of the faith community will come within God's Reign if they submit to the Good News. Oftentimes, they will be members without realizing it. See Matthew 25: 38-46, where Jesus says that when he was hungry, thirsty, a stranger, naked, sick, in prison, you ministered to me. When asked when all these things happened, He responded, "When you did it to the least of my people, you did it unto me."

Next for Matthew, living in the Reign of God does not involve strict adherence to certain rules and regulations, as if this is viewed as an end in itself. To say, "I have not missed a day of Sunday School or a worship service in my entire life" does not mean anything if the person has no God awareness outside the confines of the local church building. In speaking of the local religious authorities, He says:

> The scribes and the Pharisees have succeeded Moses as teachers; therefore, do everything and observe everything they tell you. But do not follow their example. Their words are bold but their deeds are few. They bind up heavy loads, hard to carry, to lay on other men's shoulders, while they themselves will not lift a finger to budge them.

Religion and true spirituality are not about controlling people or putting ourselves above others, but about the business of liberation and lifting others up, so they, too, may embrace all that God would have them to be. If our worship and our religion do not lead us in this direction, then we have truly misunderstood the life that the Reign of God calls us to embrace.

From his Sermon on the Mount, Jesus is recorded as saying:

> Many will plead with me, Lord, Lord have we not prophesized in your name? Have we not exorcised demons by its power? Did we not do many miracles in your name as well? Then I will declare to them solemnly, I never knew you. Out of my sight you evildoers! (7: 22-23) (*Paraphrase by RLF*)

The warning that Jesus was giving may be called a "reality check." To paraphrase this teaching, He was saying: "You have not arrived; you have just started! This is an open window to new possibilities for the Community of Faith and the Kingdom of God."

The "Kingdom of Heaven" and the "Kingdom of God" are identical terms referring to God's people. In Matthew's understanding of Jesus, the will of God, the name of God, and the presence of God mean the same thing. Becoming a person under that power will continually entail a process of becoming that which God intended one to be.

The authority and reign of God's saving presence for Matthew were present in the person of Jesus. A sign of the in-breaking of the Messianic Presence would be the "forgiveness of sin," which both John the Baptist and Jesus proclaimed. The name of Mary's baby established his identity as this saving authority of God, inaugurating God's Reign of Salvation.

In the person of Jesus, God inaugurated a new dimension of the Divine Presence. Jesus was the manifestation of what it means to be a person under God's rule. He gave evidence of this through His teaching, preaching, and healing among the poor and the sick.

While the Jewish population had "messianic expectations" that would bring a radical reordering of all structures of society and its institutions, they were unable to detect the messianic presence in the life and work of this Jesus from Nazareth. Their preconceived ideas got in the way. They knew what the Kingdom of God looked like, so they were assured that when they saw it, they would recognize it. It didn't happen! They looked for a warrior like David who would once again bring the nation back to its days of glory. This guy from Nazareth did not fit the bill.

Since God's plan was essentially related to the inclusion of those very people who were being excluded and the non-violent method that is a key component to Jesus' style of ministry, He appeared to be nothing like David. So He was rejected by the religious authorities of His day.

The Reverend Dr. Martin Luther King embraced the non-violent style of reform for all people of color, which included whites as well. Social change does not come easy. Old habits are hard to break, but the battle still goes on today. While the power of social norms is unrelenting, the Kingdom of God is stronger and more powerful. If it is truly the will of God that all of humanity be treated with equal rights and opportunities, so it will be.

Thus, the Kingdom of God is about people and meeting the needs of people. It is not about getting, but about the act of giving. Not about what we can collect, but what we are willing to give away. The symbol that best represents the Kingdom of God is the inverted pyramid. The goal of the Kingdom of God is not upper mobility, but downward service to humanity.

Is there a place in your life for the Kingdom of God?

THE UNEXPECTED

All of the family was excited and getting ready for their annual trip to the mountains. Everyone would be going, including Grandpa and Grandma. Oh yes! We can't forget the new addition to the family, a small Labrador puppy. The mountains are always a good place to kick back and enjoy the moment.

A few days into the vacation, despite everyone in the campground's being alerted, the Labrador puppy cannot be found. Not that far away on a lonely mountain slope, a small Labrador puppy continued to scramble, but without success. It seems that the puppy was unable to scale the last foot and a half of the slope because of the vertical angle. On each attempt, he rolled back and then over, to try again.

In a zoo far, far away, a bluebird had fallen into one of the big pools, where the weight of the water on its wings made flight impossible. Undaunted, the bird continued to flap its wings in an attempt to fly, but soon was exhausted.

A puppy! A bird! Both were in a life-threatening situation. Many before them had died. Would this be their fate? It is obvious that without help they will die.

So as Paul Harvey would often say, "Here is the rest of the story."

Back on the mountaintop in Tennessee, a cat that had wondered away from the campsite, sat perched at the top of the mountain slope. She watched as the puppy tried again and again to navigate to the top. Exhausted with watching the puppy's efforts, the cat decided to take matters into her own paws. She leapt down the slope, grabbed the puppy by the nap of the neck and with great effort dragged him up the vertical incline, the last foot and a half, where no puppy had ever gone before. The cat's intervention saved the life of the puppy. Who would ever think that a cat would rescue a puppy?

Meanwhile, back at the zoo, a nose began to emerge from the great pool of water at the point where the bluebird floated. As the nose came up higher and higher, it was apparent the bird was sitting on top, with its wings being slowly dried by the sun. Soon the little creature tentatively flapped its wings to expel the water that remained and then launched itself into the awaiting sky. Who would ever think that a hippo would come to the rescue of a drowning bird?

These two stories from the animal world are true; the names have been changed to protect the innocent. If animals can do the unexpected, why can't we human beings? Why can't we step outside our comfort zones and do the right thing? What is expected of us is to hate our neighbor who has wronged us in some way or another. We are expected to take revenge on those who have hurt us! To be suspicious of people who are different from us!

The fourth chapter of the Gospel according to John records a day in the life of Jesus. He and his disciples are on their way to Galilee and are passing through Samaria, where the half-breeds live. Those who have chosen to marry outside their community are not accepted by either Samarians or Jews. They are the half-breeds. The undesirables of the world!

So near the village of Sychar, at Jacob's well, it is mid-afternoon. A Samarian woman is filling her amphora, having chosen this time because she is not welcomed at the well in the morning when it is typical for women to come. It is in this place and under these circumstances that she runs into Jesus, who asks her for a drink of water. She knows He is from the better side of the tracks, and discerns that He is not blind. She wonders, a bit fearful: " My own people won't have anything to do with me, so why has this Jewish gentleman asked of me a cup of water?"

The answer is a rather simple one. Jesus saw the equality of all people. All people come from God and eventually all people return to God. Every human being is stamped with the Imago Dei (the Image of God). This impression is not just a spiritual marking, but occupies every nook and cranny in what we describe as being human. God is in every human life. There is no such thing as being "Godless." The basic struggle for human beings is not how to get God in our lives, but to discover the presence of God who is already there, knocking from the inner soul, inviting us to come into the inner sanctuary of our being.

Unfortunately, the presence of God in every human life is often hidden behind the walls of prejudice, nationalism, ethnic association and religion. It is one thing to be patriotic, but it is another thing to take this concept to the point that one believes God loves us more than any other nation in the world. Remember there are Third World Nations because there are third-rate human beings governing and a third-rate corporate mindset that takes advantage of such people. I realize that there were slave traders on both sides of the ocean. Neither is innocent in the eyes of God. I use the present tense because oppression is still alive and well in our world

.

When will all this end? Not until the supreme desire for self-gain, power and control are abated. The Old Testament prophets confronted the leaders of the Northern Kingdom and the Southern Kingdom to tell them they should turn away from their selfish ways, do what is right (justice) and liberate the oppressed. No stone was left unturned and no one was excused from the demands on the nation and all of people. It mattered not to the prophets were the chips fell. Whether in the lap of the king, the high priests, or merchants in the marketplace, all had a responsibility to do justice and liberate the oppressed.

The Book of James says that we can't say we love God and treat our fellow human beings unjustly. The two concepts do not mix. When we do this, we do not please God.

So, what say you?   Can you do the unexpected?

THE VILLAGE

Grace Cotton Mill Village, located in the foothills of Western North Carolina, was a great place to live and grow up. There were kids to play games and ride bicycles with. We used the old cow pasture down the road as our baseball field in the summer and touch football field in the fall. Life was good!

My parents paid rent of $1.00 a month, which included water, for our four-room house with a huge front porch, which was just the right size for several rocking chairs and a swing. When the house needed painting, or anything else, the work was provided by the mill maintenance crew at no charge.

It has been said that all good things must come to an end, and so it was with life in the mill village. In the fall of 1957, I said good-bye to my 7th grade class at Ruth Elementary School. Grace Cotton Mill was closing down due to a recession, which at the time I knew nothing about. We were moving to Spartanburg, SC, because my father was being transferred to another Reeves Brothers' Plant. It was sad to leave my friends, but it was also exciting to be moving to another state.

We moved to a place I considered out in the middle of nowhere, about five or six miles from Valley Falls, where I finished out my 7th grade. It was most difficult coming in in the middle of a school year and being so far behind the other kids. In just a month or so, I would be taking mid-term exams.

Over the Christmas Holidays I studied each and every day, trying to catch up on South Carolina his-tory and the Swamp Fox and a band of other characters I knew very little about. My best efforts were not good enough; the highest grade on the mid-term exams for me was a C on English. Everything else was downhill from there! My teacher told my parents if I passed my final exams, he would pass me to the 8th grade. Somehow, someway, I pulled it off.

Many, many years later I decided to take another trip through the Grace Cotton Mill Village for old times' sake. Boy was I in for a shock! Both houses that I grew up in were gone. The old cow pasture where we played baseball and football had trees, bushes and a lot of other things growing everywhere. You would never believe that there was once a "home plate" out there somewhere. Junky cars were everywhere, and the houses that were still standing looked as though they were ready to fall in. The village I knew growing up was gone.

In spite of the changes, there were some lessons to be learned. One: life is not standing still! We live in a linear world, and there are no second chances to do life over. The choices we have made are final, so the best we can do is accept the past for what it was and what it may teach us. In the 60s, Dusty Springfield recorded "Wishing & Hoping." Wishing that our past had been different and that we had made better choices will get us nowhere. Remember that there are some important choices still ahead of us.

We need to decide what we want to do with the rest of our lives. The past is what it is behind us. Some memories are good, some are bad! We live with both, with the hope that we will do better in the present moment. There is an old saying, "Live and Learn." We need to appreciate the past for the lessons it taught us. We need to look at all our failures, hardships, and struggles from a positive point of view — we survived. Yes, in spite of all that happened in our past, somehow, someway we survived. So we are survivalists and that's not bad!

The cotton mill village is gone. The old home place is gone. The places where we gathered are gone. Old friends are gone. What is all of this saying to us? Don't let the past cheat you out of the present moment. If we go through life looking back, we miss the present moment which is all we have in life. There are some things about which we need to take the attitude that our past was what it was and there is nothing we can change about it. In spite of what happened or didn't happen in our past, the question that we want to consider is what are we going to do with the rest of our lives?

In spite of what has been done to you and taken from you, what do you still have that you can give back to your family, place of worship, and community? Remember it is in the act of giving our life away that we find life and it is the attempt to hold onto our life that causes us to lose it. So let go of what could have been and embrace the possibilities. If we do this, we may end up doing something we never thought we could do.

Can you let go of your negative past and embrace the present possibilities for your life?

THROWING PETALS

She was only four or five years old at the time, but she had an awesome responsibility that day. As flower girls in a wedding, she and another little girl were to distribute flower petals down the church aisle before the bride-to-be made her way to the front of the church. Teresa Gail Newton took this task very seriously, and she expected the other little girl to do the same. In Gail's mind there was an ordered way to do this, so when she saw the other little girl throwing petals everywhere, she had to step in and set her straight — in the best stern voice she could muster. I don't know if the little girl caught on to Gail's technique or not, but at least she would know for future reference.

You need to know that Gail's background is German. Apparently a pretty strong bloodline! I have been married to her for 42 years, and I can tell you that in the process of growing up, she did not leave this rigid view of life behind. It has been a tough life for her, living with the "loosey-goosey" type of guy that I am. You know, they say opposites attract. Gail has always been a person who pays a lot of attention to detail. When she takes on a task, she does it the best it can be done. People like me need people like Gail to keep us on the straight and narrow. I am a visionary type of person. I can describe the vision, but I can't tell you how to make it happen. Given time and resources, she *can* make it happen. We need people around us that know how to get things done.

With this thought in mind, I find very interesting the variety of people that Jesus picked to be on his God Mission Team. At least four were fishermen, one a tax collector, one an accountant, plus six others from various backgrounds. I suppose what bothers me about this is that he did not choose any women. Leonardo da Vinci did not place any women in his painting of the Last Supper. Still, they were involved in the life and ministry of Jesus. Randel Lolley, former president of the Southeastern Baptist Theological Seminary in Wake Forest, NC, once preached a sermon in our chapel service with the title, "Last at the Cross, First at the Tomb." It was a sermon about Mary Magdalene. It is believed by many scholars that she was the woman at the well whom Jesus met, when his disciples had gone into town to get food. Being first at the tomb meant that she was the first person to preach the Gospel to the disciples. Strange turn of events!

Maybe the absence of women mentioned by the Gospel writers was more about the attitude of the writers than the mind and disposition of Jesus. As James Brown informs us in his song, "It's A Man's World," this has certainly been the case not only in the days and times of Jesus. Even today it is hard for women to break into what has been known as a "man's world." The TV shows back in the '50s certainly showed us where women ought to be — at home and in the kitchen. This was the case for Beaver Cleaver's mom and Harriet of "Ozzie and Harriet," as well as June of "Father Knows Best."

I am reminded that in one of Paul's letters he says: "There is neither Jew nor Greek; there is neither slave nor free; nor is there male and female, for you are all one in Christ Jesus." Galatians 3:28 (*KJV*) Well, he certainly said a mouthful. What does all this mean? My personal view is that Paul is saying God is color blind and gender blind. If this is true, then Paul made a very bold statement in the midst of a very male-dominated society.

Therefore, God will call whomever He wants to call to do His work in the world. What I take from this is that women can be preachers or deacons in a church, political leaders, corporate CEOs, or perform any other job that is normally held by men. While I am not Catholic, I believe that women ought to be allowed to be priests and maybe someday a woman will become Pope. Women's struggle for justice continues. Quite frankly, I hope the women win the struggle.

The important thing in life is that you pursue the destiny that God has designed for you. Be what God wants you to be, not what society says you must be. You will find it most gratifying.

Are you free to throw petals God's way?

TOUCHED BY AN ANGEL

It was a typical Sunday morning in this quaint southern town in the foothills of Western North Carolina. The churchgoers filled the highways and byways, as they traveled to their appointed places of worship. In the midst of all this activity, there was one car that was not moving. Something had gone wrong with this car, and now it was sitting quietly beside the road. Two adults and two teenaged children stood looking as the traffic passed them by.

Usually there is some "Good Samaritan" who will stop to assist a family in distress, but not this day. Maybe it was the way they were dressed that caused some concern for those who thought about stopping to help. Their outward appearance gave the hint of someone connected to the Middle East. So the thought that may have traveled through the minds of the ministers, deacons, and other church folks was that the members of this family were not "one of us."

So there they sat, watching as car after car whizzed by. Then they heard someone coming through the bushes that lined the road. It was a middle-aged, homeless man who had spent the night out in the woods and was now on his way to a nearby convenience store. It so happens that this man had been a master mechanic in his good days before drugs took control of his life. He was able to correct the problem with the car, so the grateful family gave him a ride to the convenience store.

This was quite an interesting scene! Here was a family who had come upon some bad luck, but no one would stop to help them. Enter a man who is down on his luck with only the woods to call home. Neither is fully accepted by the community in which they live. They are outsiders! Not our kind of people! You can't trust them!

It is ironic that as the churchgoers zoomed by on their way to find God, they passed Him by. Remember the scripture that says when you help someone who is going through a difficult time, you can consider that you have done it to and for God. Sometimes God is found in unfamiliar places in life and in the lives of unfamiliar people. It seems to me that a lot of folks are in a hurry to get from point A to point C and in the process miss the blessing that may be found at point B.

Eckhart Tolle in his book, *The New Earth*, reminds us that if life is a journey, and the challenge is to embrace each and every moment as we move through it. This involves the earth that surrounds us, as well as the people and creatures who cross our pathway. Remember also the scripture that points out how we often entertain angels (God's messengers) unaware.

Such was the case for Jacob as he spent his first night away from home in the desert. He had a dream that night with angels going up and down a large ramp connecting heaven and earth. When he awoke the next morning, he made this profound statement: "God was in this place and I knew it not." This experience came at the right time for him. It was a reminder that in his aloneness, God was present and active. When he needed it the most, he was touched by an angel and given the energy to continue his journey.

The family with the broken down automobile found their angel in the form of a homeless man. He came out of the woods just at the right time and place. This was no accident; it was by Divine design.

Been touched by an angel?

TRANSITIONS

The anticipation and excitement were building up as the creatures stood looking at the great gulf that lay between them and the other side of the river, a place they called home. It was the day and time for the huge herd of wildebeest to make their way across this treacherous span of water. The river was swarming with these larger-than-life reptilians. The crocodiles ruled the river, but the crossing had to be made. It was time to go to greener pastures where grass was in abundance. Eventually, one wildebeest would test the waters and then another until the whole herd was making its way down the embankment. There were losses, but the sacrifice of a few made it possible for the majority to make it.

It was the Preacher from the Old Testament who reminds us that life has its seasons. Each season of life has its own challenges. The season of birth and death are not an intrusion, but a part of our journey. We plant and we harvest. We give life away and we receive life. We build and we tear down. We laugh and we cry. We mourn the passing of life, and we celebrate the giving of life with laughter and rejoicing. We leave and we return. We throw away and we collect. We destroy and we repair. We talk a lot and sometimes we listen. We love and we hate. We make war and we seek peace. (*From Proverbs 3: 1-9. Paraphrase by RLF*)

Transitions are never easy. Fear, uncertainty, and doubt cause us to ask, "Should I really do this or is there another way that is better?" The scriptures tell us that each one of us must work out her or his own salvation. The reason God never leaves or forsakes us is that He can't trust us out in this big world on our own. We need His help.

Going through some transitions in your life? Trust God!

WE'RE IN THIS TOGETHER

They preached and wrote from the heart! No stone was left unturned! The message was straightforward and focused on all the people near and far. No one was excluded. Such was the intent and purpose of the prophetic voice among the people of God. It was consistent with the former voices that resonated through the hills and valleys. The bottom line was always the same, "We're in this together." What goes on with one goes on with all.

It started with dry bones and ended up with a multitude of people fully covered with clothing from the exclusive store of God Wear. You couldn't get it anywhere else! This clothing was unique in its style, and in the impression it made on all who tried it on for size. No, one size did not fit all! It was tailormade for each individual. In fact, no one could wear the clothing that was made for another person. It would not fit! Each Divine Representative of God would have his or her own calling and purpose that would fit perfectly into the puzzle of the whole multitude. Different, yet joined together in a common purpose.

He was minding his own business one day when a stranger showed up at his doorstep. As was the custom of the day, he offered the man the best of hospitality. Before long the stranger said, "Come with me. I have something I want to show you."

There was a manner about this stranger that compelled him to put down his work, grab his coat and follow. Curiosity had gotten the best of him, so turning back was not an option. He knew the terrain, so there was nothing out there that he had not seen before, but maybe today it would be different.

Indeed it was. Down below him in a valley deep and wide lay the remains of a multitude of people. Nothing but bones! As far as the eye could see, nothing but bones. The stranger asked quietly: "Do you see what I see?"

Somewhat sheepishly, he answered: "Yes. It is a valley full of bones that have been there for a long, long time. I can't believe that I did not see them before."

"Not to worry," said the stranger. "These bones are only visible at certain times and under certain conditions. Now, this is what I want you to do for me, as odd as it may seem to you, I want you to preach to these dry bones. Preach life into them, that these dry bones may once again become the people of God. Would you do that for me?" Then he stepped back slowly, as if to say, "The show is in your hands!"

There come those times in life when it seems that the task at hand is totally out of reach. When deep down we know that whatever our solution, it won't work.

We have called in all the king's horses and all the king's men, but they have declined to attempt to put all this back together again. Better to go on to something more manageable!

Preach to these dry bones and leave the results to God? Well, under these circumstances, the preacher would do what he could.

Sometimes the hardest part of a project is getting started! The fear of trying keeps whispering in your ears, "This can't be done! It's a waste of your time and effort. Cut your losses! Just slowly walk away."

This might be easy for some, but not for the preacher. This was what he was called to do, so how could he just walk away? He would never know what might happen, so he had to at least give it his best effort.

Somewhere in the world, the movement of the Spirit of God goes unnoticed, but not in this place. As the preacher stepped forward, cleared his voice, and spoke "Thus sayeth the Lord," a marvelous thing took place in the valley below. The bones began to come together, and there before him were thousands and thousands of human skeletons throughout the valley. As he continued to preach, muscle and tendons began to form all over the skeletons. Next, skin began to grow and develop. Soon there were complete human bodies throughout the valley, but no life in them.

"Command the Spirit to blow upon them and bring life to their lungs and body," said the stranger. As the preacher continued, he heard a great wind rushing down the mountain sides into the valley. Soon the Wind blew upon, around, and within each and every person there. The people began to walk around; they started to dance and sing praises to the Most High God. The voices rose up in unison. That which had been dead had come to life. It was a transformation to behold. It all came forth out of the will and purpose of God for his people. It was an act of God's creative power. Not one single soul was left out! The body was complete. Not a single person missing in action. All were accounted for and present.

In a less dramatic way, this takes place in the weekly worship event across our nation and around the world. The demands of the preceding week have taken their toll upon the spiritual life of God's people. These dry bones assemble in their designated places; some with very little expectation that anything new will happen and hoping to endure the hourly event.
But each and every week there is a mystery at work among the gathering clan. They have come as individuals, but in the joining of the congregation, they have become one body before God. It is not evident, but true, and you know that what happens to one part of the body impacts the whole body.

The Apostle Paul puts this into perspective in First Corinthians 12: 12-26:

> The body is one, yet it has many members that work together. Such is the Body of Christ! As our body has many component parts, yet it is one body, such is the Body of

Christ. The foot cannot claim that because it is not a hand that it is not a part of the body, it is. Nor can the ear say that because it is not an eye that it is not part of the body, for it is. For if the whole body was an ear or an eye, what would become of the body's ability to eat or drink? God has placed the various members together as he decided, but each functions together as one body. So then, if one member suffers, all the other members suffer with it. When one member receives special treatment, all the members rejoice. (*Paraphrase by RLF*)

When food comes into the body, the whole body benefits. When air enters the lungs, the whole body receives its benefits. If you are a member of the body you get it. This is automatic. No paperwork needed!

Therefore, what happens to one member of the congregation happens to all. The choir sings praises to God, which becomes our praise to God. Someone prays an uplifting prayer; it, too, is our prayer to God. What happens to one, happens to all. God pours out his blessings upon his people irregardless of how they feel or think. Because you are part of the Body of Christ, you get it. You cannot not get it! What you do with it is another thing altogether.

The next time you go to your place of worship and take your seat where you normally do, remember that while you come as an individual, you have now joined the congregation. The God who formed the world and universe has formed this gathering. What happens to one, happens to all. Why?

Because, we are all in this together!

WHEN GOD WINKS

Augh, just what I always wanted, a root canal! I assure you this was not on my bucket-list. My regular dentist referred me to an oral surgeon to have this procedure performed. I was given a prescription for medication, which I took — as instructed — an hour before my appointment, to make sure I would not be in pain.

As I sat in the waiting area outside the surgeon's office, the medication began to hit home. Slowly I made my way to the floor, sliding out of my chair as the medication overcame my ability to remain seated. I have no remembrance of what happened next. My wife asked if someone on the staff could help her get me off the floor, but was told that no one was available to help. So there I lay on the floor of the waiting room, out like a light. What to do? My wife was running out of options.

Sometimes there is a "God Winks at You Moment" in life. This was one of those days. In the Sunday School

Class I teach each week is a gentleman whose name is Dennis Hege. Dennis works for a local telephone company, and on this particular day he was doing some work at the dentist's office where I lay on the floor. When Dennis walked into the waiting area, my wife quickly enlisted him to help her get me into the car. Fortunately, Dennis is a well-built, strong man, so they succeeded in getting me to the car. The next problem was how to get me into my house. Gail called her father to help, and somehow they managed to get me to my bedroom with very little bruising. I have no remembrance of what went on that day or the next day either.

Eventually, another appointment was made, and the root canal was a success. The medication dosage was reduced, so I was able to move around on my own power. It was an experience my wife would like to forget, and one I have very little remembrance of, but we both recognize that in the middle of all the stress and confusion, God placed Dennis right where we needed him to be. Some folks would say that in this world we have good luck and bad luck. We never know which one we will end up with, but it will be one or the other. The Judeo-Christian perspective does not subscribe to the element of luck, but rather Divine Intervention. Think about it for a moment: were the people who came in contact with the historical Jesus just lucky, or was there a much larger plan at work that no one knew anything about?

We are told that God works in mysterious ways, His wonders to behold. Is it not possible that God is at work in every moment of our lives to take us from where we are to where we need to be?

Has God winked at you today?

WHERE ARE YOU GOING?

On a Sunday afternoon, in the summer of 1862, the Reverend Charles Lutwidge Dodgson and the Reverend Robinson Duckworth rowed a boat up the River Thames with the three young daughters of Henry Liddell, who was the Vice-Chancellor of Oxford University and Dean of Christ Church. The journey began at Folly Bridge near Oxford and ended five miles away in the village of Godstow. During the trip, one of the girls asked the Reverend Dodgson to tell them a story. So began a story that would later be known as *Alice in Wonderland*, written by Lewis Carroll.

At one point in the story, Alice meets up with the Cheshire Cat at a place in her journey through Wonderland where the road goes in all directions. When Alice asks the Cat, which way she should go, the Cat answers, "Where do you want to go?"

Alice replies, "I really don't know!"

The Cat responds, "Well, it really doesn't matter which road you take."

Those of us who have been around for a while have in many ways been given an answer to that question, but that's not true for many just out of high school and college, who haven't a clue as to which road to take.

Some of my classmates were signing up for classes at the new community technical college in Spartanburg, South Carolina, so with nothing better else to do, I signed up too. Two years later I graduated with an Associate of Science Degree in Electronic Technology and found myself in the same situation again; which road should I take now? At the time the Military Draft was in full swing, so some of my friends were going into the Air Force. With nothing better else to do, I joined the Air Force too. Four years later, at the end of my tour of duty, I was at another crossroad, again faced with the decision of which road to take. I had made the rank of Staff Sergeant and would qualify as a VRB-4 if I signed up for another tour of duty. That meant that I could receive four times my annual salary in one lump sum, which would amount to over $8,000. A lot of money was looking me in the face, but in spite of this large amount money for me in the year of 1968, I turned it down and went back home. At that time some of my friends were working at Western Electric, so I got a job there, too. Six months later I quit my job with no particular place to go. So, back to the crossroads once again!

For some reason I decided to go to a school in Atlanta, GA, to get my First Class FCC License. This would allow me to work at a radio or TV station. Six months later with my First Class FCC License in hand, I was back at the crossroads one more time. Later on, I put my application in at WSPA-TV Spartanburg, SC, and bingo, I got a job. To my surprise, I would not be working at the local studio as I had thought I would be, but at the top of Hogback Mountain, which was located in northern Greenville County, S.C.

Sometimes there comes a yearning in the depth of our soul that causes a discomfort that seems to spread over our entire world. After two years into my work on Hogback Mountain the thrill was gone. There had to be something that I was more fitted to do. I didn't know or even have a clue as to what that something was or where to find it.

One day, when I returned home from work, my mother told me that an insurance company had called about a job for me. The person told my mom that I had come highly recommended for the job, and they would like an interview with me. Boy what timing! Just the night before I had asked God to show me what he wanted me to do with my life, and now I knew.

The appointment was made, and off I went to become an insurance salesman. I have to say that there was some fear and trembling on my part about making a good impression. The interview went great, and the job offer was made. All I had to do now was take a physical exam and attend some training classes and I would be good to go.

A few days later I was in the office of a local doctor who provided this service for the company. Since it had been just a few years since I was discharged from the Air Force, I knew that there would be no problem passing the physical. After all the tests had been performed, the doctor came back in and announced that he had some bad news for me. It seems that he heard a heart murmur and wanted to know if I had ever had rheumatic fever.

Knowing that this was God's will for me life, I felt it necessary to tell a small, little lie. "No, I don't believe I have," was my response. Of course I knew that I had been diagnosed with rheumatic fever three times in my life.

The next day the insurance company informed me that they could not hire me with a heart murmur. It was devastating news. How could they turn me down? This was what God had called me to do. This made no sense to me. No doctor had heard that heart murmur in years, so why was it back again?

A few days later, I went to my family doctor to have it checked out. Over and over again he listened to my heart, ran an EKG, took my BP, put me on a treadmill and doing jumping-jacks. If there was a heart murmur it would show up, but it didn't. As best he tried, the doctor could not hear a heart murmur. He gave me a clean bill of health. I had done all I could do, so it was up to God to come up with something. Feeling some sense of disappointment, I continued my work at Hogback Mountain; accepting that was where I needed to be.

In the lonely hours of being at the transmitter site, and somewhere around the hour of 2:00 a.m. when the TV transmitter was shut down for the night until 5:00 a.m., there came a voice to me in that silence. Whether the voice came from within me or from someplace else, I do not know. But I do know that it was crystal clear. No static! The voice addressed me personally, "Robert Loran Ford, I have called you to the work of ministry." At times like this you begin to wonder if the voice was all a dream or was it real. Maybe it was both!

This voice had come to me while I was in Technical College, so I ran from it by joining the Air Force. Now it was back again! I'm between a rock and a hard place: while I can't say no, I can't say yes either. I'm stuck! How can I get away from this? I don't want God to make a mistake a second time. I felt like the hare in Francis Thompson's epic poem, **"The Hound of Heaven."** It depicts God's chase of pursu-ing His own that seeks to escape His embrace. God will not let up nor will he give up the chase until His will and purpose have been fulfilled.

But how could God keep on making the same mistake? He should know that the one thing that I'm not good at is public speaking. I hate it! I'd rather have a root canal done than make a public presentation. What I know about the Bible you could put in a thimble and still have room left over. I remember how hard it was for me to give an oral book report in my English class in high school. This would be like giving an oral book report every week. There was no way that I could handle that. I raised the issue that I couldn't do anything without training.

Eventually I quit making excuses and said yes to my calling from God. I discovered that the direction was not mine to choose, but mine to travel as directed by the Great Navigator. I discovered that God was able to see more in me than I could. I have been amazed at what He has accomplished in my life. I could not even imagine it at that time, but God could, and that made all the difference.

It seems never to be a simple process. As the Old Testament Prophets struggled with their calling, it's okay for you to struggle with yours. It's okay to doubt yourself, and it's okay to doubt God's ability to accomplish his work through you. This is part of the process that leads to the path not yet traveled. It all leads to acceptance and acceptance to action.

At this point in your life, **"Where Are You Going?"**

WHERE IN THE WORLD IS GOD?

> In the beginning. . . .the earth was not. The universe was void. It did not exist. There was nothing but darkness and in the darkness was God. All that existed was God. There was nothing, but God. God filled the nothing. The Nothing and God were the same since nothing else existed. Out of the nothing God spoke." Genesis 1:1-3a (*Paraphrase by RLF*)

The most powerful entity in the universe is God. In the beginning God was in the nothing and the nothing was in God. So, how close is God to us? Look around and everywhere you see nothing, there is God. The space between the molecules in your body is where God exists. Truly God is everywhere and there is no space that God does not fill. The Psalmist asks the question: "How can I escape from God? If I go into the highest heavens, God is there. If I go to the deepest part of hell, God is there."

The standard procedure for having a relationship with God is to ask God to come into our lives. While this has been in vogue for hundreds of years, to my way of thinking it should be the other way around.

First of all, one of my basic beliefs about God is that He is always where He needs to be. Second, it is you and I who are so often not where we need to be, physically, mentally, and spiritually in relation with God. We need to make an adjustment and be in God's life, since God's life is already within us. We need to take a journey into ourselves to discover God and who we are.

In Revelation 3:11, we find these words: "Behold I stand at the door and knock." The most common interpretation is that our Lord is standing outside our door requesting to come in. I take a different view: it is our Lord who is already inside this life inviting us to come in to Him.

Saint Augustine said that to know God was to know ourselves. Simply put, self-discovery is not easy. Therefore we need someone to help guide us and help us understand all that we are experiencing.

I have been fortunate to have had some very insightful people in my life who have helped me to understand myself and to better understand what God is up to in my life. I did my CPE (Clinical Pastoral Education) through Baptist Hospital in Winston-Salem, NC. My supervisor was John Edgerton. Through his work with me, I discovered more about why I do certain things I do.

Later on a friend of mine, Chaplain Cindy Jordon, introduced me to a group of chaplains in a CPSP

(Clinical Pastoral Supervision and Psychotherapy) setting. We met four or five times each year for a two-day session in which each member had to tell something about her or his life story. Gene Rollins and Hayden Howell were two of the most engaging members for me. I have always thought of myself as being on the dumb side of life. The group helped me to accept the creative and imaginative parts of my life. Like the Scarecrow in the Wizard of Oz, I discovered I had a brain.

At the ripe old age of 74 ½, I am still digging through the rubble discovering more things about myself and about my Lord. Such writers as Jean Varnier, Henry Nouwen, and Markus Borg, to name a few, have helped me in my journey of self-discovery. I like books that challenge my way of thinking and my world view and thereby offer me the best opportunity to grow and develop all that God has provided me.

I now have a better understanding of the Creation Story. "The Lord God formed mankind out of the dust of the ground, and breathed into their nostrils the breath of life; and mankind became living beings." Genesis 2:7 (KJV) The Hebrew word for wind is "Ruah," the same word that is used describe the movement and activity of God. Thus we could say the "Wind of God" or the "Spirit of God." Life comes from this breath of God. Imagine, with each and every breath, we breathe in the good stuff, the Ruah, and we exhale the bad stuff, which the Ruah of God carries from our body.

Where in the world is God in your life? Maybe closer than you think!

WHO AM I?

How did all this happen? One day you are in a safe environment, surrounded by everything you will ever need and then it happens—you have a coming-into-the-world day. Someone grabs you, holds you upside down and pronounces you to be a boy or a girl. You are given a name, whether you like it or not. You then spend the rest of your life trying to put meaning to the name.

The first struggle before us is control. The first challenge is with our body and then our mind. The spiritual dimension seems to come last. At some point we discover that life is not fair. There has not been an equal distribution of resources in the universe. Some run faster, jump higher, and excel in areas of life that provide a wealth of resources and opportunities.

Some move to the top of the mountain and others find their way into the valley below. Of course, there are those who remain somewhere in the middle, which is not a bad place to be.

In either case, the task is determining your destiny, which will in many ways help you discover who you are. What kind of person do you want to be? What do you want to do with your life? Tough questions with no easy answers! For some it is easier to follow than to lead, so they just go with the flow. This is not always bad, if you keep in mind that you have the right to change your mind and go in another direction.

The Bible seems to imply that we need to leave home if we want to find home. Many adventuresome young souls have gone out to set the world on fire, only to return home to get more matches. It is not an easy matter breaking away from the place that has been the source of our well-being, but it needs to happen.

Scripture says that, "A man shall leave his father and mother, and shall cleave to his wife; and they shall be one flesh." Genesis 2: 24 (*Paraphrase by RLF*) The question is, which one will they become? Time will tell, you say, or will at least provide some clue. But what if, before they could get the plane off the ground, it crashed? Some would say it is only matter of time before trouble comes into a relationship. One bad decision leads to another and then another until a bottom is reached. It is at the bottom of the mountain where the valley lies and all you can do is look up. The sun does not shine in these places. The darkness is so thick that you can cut it with a knife. It is the place where all hope is gone.

No this place is not hell, or maybe it is! Let me say that it is as close to hell as you can get on Earth. The downhill spiral that led to this Godforsaken place derives from what has become known as the "Seven Deadly Sins:" **avarice** (the greed for wealth and the unwillingness to share our prosperity), **envy** (being obsessed with what someone else has to the point that you cannot have a healthy relationship with the person), **wrath** (a strong vengeful anger that seeks to destroy another person), **sloth** (lazy to the point of not participating in one's own well-being or that of others), **lust** (looking upon another person as an object to satisfy our desires), **gluttony** (excessive eating and drinking), and **pride** (to think more highly of ourselves than we ought to). I stand guilty of all! There are more that I have not counted, but they're just as deadly.

There is something missing, and I cannot for the life of me put my finger on it. It is something that everybody else has, but I don't. I was absent the day it was handed out. Self-confidence has not been a strong factor in my life. There is a voice that says I'm not good enough, no matter how hard I try. Make no mistake about it, I have received healing words of how good I am, but I don't believe it. I can't believe it, because it would destroy my cover.

Crazy as it may seem, I hide from myself. The dark side of me washes upon my life like a tidal wave. It brings thoughts that will not go away no matter what I do. I try music, which works sometimes and sometimes not. Some thoughts come and go and some take up residency. I should charge rent, or maybe I should pay rent.

Where did I pick up all this crazy stuff? I'm hyperactive and I have attention deficit disorder. This does not make me a good student. In fact, I was the student from hell. Never in my seat! Always bugging the other students with my attempts to be funny! I always thought it was them, but it was me. Somehow I missed this. I suppose it was easier to blame someone else for my behavior than to take ownership. If someone else owns it, then it is their responsibility to do something with it, not mine.

While there are some things embedded in my personality over which I have little control, some behaviors I do have some control over. It is this part of me that I need to wrestle with. Talking too much at times! Not talking at all! I'm not consistent. I can't wait for my turn to speak, so I just blurt out what I'm thinking. Over the years I have really gotten good at this. In fact, I would say that I am borderline expert in this field. Better to be good at something or maybe not!

Making up my mind on something is a battle! It's hard to make a decision. So many options! I want to get it right the first time, but hardly get it right anytime. Thank God I can always hide behind my humor. Good or bad, it seems to work! If I can just walk away while everyone is feeling okay about themselves, I'm free. Still, it does get old trying to figure all this stuff out and put it into proper perspective.

Well, I'm not alone! The Apostle Paul spoke of his dilemma in Romans 7. Two natures are at work in Paul and it is here that the battle takes place. He says:

> What I find myself doing, I do not understand why I'm doing it. I find myself doing what I don't like to do, but I'm doing it anyway. In fact, I hate some of the things I find myself doing, but can't seem to stop. I know that something has gone amuck that lives in me and so often controls me. I feel at times that nothing good dwells within me. In spite of my outward appearance, I'm not as good as I appear to be. There is a war going on in me, which I am forever battling. I'm up against the ropes, hanging on for dear life. How am I ever going to get out of this mess? Who can save me from myself? Is there someone who can inter-vene? Thanks be to God and the Divine Mediator who reached down into the storms of my life and lifted me above the fray. Romans 7: 14-25 (*Paraphrase by RLF*)

I am reminded of the old hymn, "Love Lifted Me," which speaks of a rescue from the angry sea. It is a song about souls in danger of being overcome by the circumstances of life. Where will their help come from? Who will care enough to take the risk of helping them in such a dangerous situation? As the song goes, it is the love of God that intervenes and by so doing brings peace into a troubled life.

We win by the grace of God. While we may give up on ourselves, God never does. Knowing what we can be and knowing what has been bestowed upon us, we are recipients of the perfect life of God. In the Gospel According to John, Jesus says that all that the Father has given to him he has in return given to us. Therefore, evil will not destroy us. The power of God to perfect us is stronger than the forces that seek to destroy us.

The story of Jacob at the River Jabbok, where he wrestles with God, has an interesting outcome. His hip is thrown out of place, but he also receives a new name — Israel. The meaning of the Hebrew word is "May God Prevail." This was not just a wish, but a reality. God's will had prevailed in his life and he would never be the same.

In his letter to the Philippians, the Apostle Paul instructs us "to let the mind of Christ be in us." What a refreshing thought! Rejoice in what God has done with us, rather than fret over what we have done to ourselves. Rejoice in the constant renewal that comes from God. Rejoice in how God sees us, rather than how we see ourselves!

To truly know who we are, we need to see ourselves the way God sees us. The Apostle Paul would often shave using a dull piece of metal, which reflected a poor image of himself. He used this experience to express how little we really know about ourselves. Paul says, "For now we see a poor image of ourselves in a mirror, but there is coming a time when we will know fully who we are in light of how God sees us." First Corinthians 13 (*Paraphrase by RLF*)

Want to know who you are? The best place to start is to discover yourself in the life and work of the historical Jesus as found in the Four Gospels. With each and every encounter, where are you in the crowd? With each story he tells, which character are you?

It is in Him — He who calls us by name — that we begin to discover who we are and our purpose and destiny in life. Then we will begin to understand our identity in light of his identity.

Do you know who you are?

WHOOPING COUGH

They made me a special place in the living room, as the family waited for the inevitable to happen! There was no known cure for what I had, so it was just a matter of time until the whooping cough would win the battle for my life. I don't know what prompted my mother to do what she did at the time, but she picked me up and took me to a small back bedroom. She lay me down on the small single bed, and as I struggled for breath, she offered me to God. Her words went something like this, "Lord, if you can use my son in any way, I give him back to you for your service. Whatever way you decide to use him, I will accept."

Sometimes in life we are surprised as to what God has in store for us. This was certainly the case with me in my sixth month of life. Apparently God accepted the terms of my mother's offer, so instead of having a graveside service for me at Southern Baptist Church, my parents watched as I began to recover. In time I was back to normal!

I did not learn of this dedication service my mother performed that day in the early summer of 1945 until the night before my graduation from seminary. Mom had kept it hidden in her heart. I suppose she had been waiting for the right moment to tell me about it. I don't think she had ever told anyone about it until she told me. I was speechless! Mom and God had planned this out a long time ago, and now it was all coming to fruition.

Even when I was off playing the part of the "Prodigal Son," Mom never gave up hope that I would eventually discover my calling from God. At some point in my education journey through college and seminary, I read the book, *The Confessions of Saint Augustine.* Certainly no one played the part of the "Prodigal Son" more than Augustine. He acknowledges that it was the prayers of his mother and her encouragement for him to turn away from his life of self-indulgence that made the difference in his life.
.

Later on in my ministry, my wife told me that when she was a baby, her mom had dedicated her life to God's service. This, too, was a private service between her mother and God. Amazing that God brought us together. I am reminded of Hannah, the mother of Samuel. When she was unable to bear a child for her husband Elkanah, she prayed to God for a child. Her prayer is given as follows:

> O Lord of hosts, if thou wilt indeed look on the affliction [unable to have children] of thine handmaid, and remember me, and not forget thine handmaid, but wilt give unto thine handmaid a child, then I will give the child unto thee, O Lord, all the days of its life.... First Samuel 1: (*Paraphrase by RLF*)

As a child, when I was hurt, I ran to Momma. Her embrace made all things right, and I found comfort in her arms. She would tell me that I would be ok. She seemed to know what I needed even before I asked. I remember one day when I was out looking through a junk pile I saw a piece of rubber hose with various colors on it. I picked it up and soon discovered that it was a snake. I quickly threw it down and ran to Momma! I wanted to know if I would die because I touched a snake. It was her embrace that assured me I would be okay.

One day, Jesus looked out at the city of Jerusalem and tenderly said of this special place in his life, "Jerusalem, Jerusalem, you have attempted to destroy all the messengers of God sent to you; but I have longed to gather you as a hen gathers her chicks under her wing, but you were not willing." Matthew 23:37 (*Paraphrase by RLF*). It is good to know that our Lord was in touch with the feminine part of his life.

The writer of the Book of Revelation gives further expression to the feminine side of God when he writes that there will be no more sea (chaos), which is a way of saying that there will be no more discord and turmoil among God's people, for those who are hurting will have God like a mother to: "wipe away all tears from their eyes; and there shall be no more death, neither sorrow, nor crying, neither shall there be any more pain: for the former things are passed away." Revelation 5:20 (*Paraphrase by RLF*)

I can't count the number of times that my mother wiped away my tears. In the middle of the night, when I had a bad dream, she would be there by my bedside to comfort me. To say that God wipes away our tears is to describe a loving and caring act of a mother. God speaks softly to us as She comforts and embraces us and wipes our tears away.

Our journey with God is made possible by someone who cares for us.

To dedicate a baby or child to God is an act of letting go and allowing God to determine the destiny of the child. Easier said than done!

Can you let go and let God choose the destiny of your child?

WOUNDED HEALERS

It was a long and winding road that led to home. Most of the weary travelers had only heard about this place from family and friends who were now dead. In fact, there were very few folks among them who had experienced the invasion and the destruction that had taken place some 70 years before. No one thought that this would have happened to them, but history proved them wrong.

They might have thought that their homecoming would be a glorious one, but that was not to be. Instead, when they finally arrived, they found most of the towns and communities lay in ruins. Their homeplace was gone. Fields that had once grown an abundance of food lay bare. The grapevines that had once been a source of nourishment and their livelihood were destroyed. There were a few cattle and goats here and there, but not enough to sustain the returning travelers. This was hardly what they had expected to find. They had heard the stories of a homeland flowing with milk and honey. A land that was abundant with crops in the field and cattle and goats galore.

The war that had broken out nearly 70 years before had devastated their homeland. Most of the people who had been captured and carried away to the foreign land were now dead, and this rag-tag bunch of pilgrims were just getting the picture of how destructive a war can be.

There are no winners in war, only survivors. Nations, families, and individuals survive the death and devastation of war and find themselves faced with the challenge of putting their lives back together. Some folks are more equipped to do this than others. Resources, influence, and political and religious clout make all the difference in the world. In most cases, either you have it or you don't. History has taught us that those who have it are far outnumbered by those who don't.

So the homecoming was filled with Fear, Uncertainty, and Doubt. I call it the FUD Factor. There are more questions than answers! More problems than solutions! More need than resources available! The devastation of the landscape reflected the inner turmoil of the people who stood gazing at a paradise lost. A way of life had been taken from them! A prevailing wind of depression blew across this gathered group of rag-tag pilgrims.

Haggai, too, was a pilgrim, and it was to this convoy of humanity that he was commissioned to bring word from the Lord. I would not have wanted to be in his shoes. Trying to bring hope and encouragement to a depressed and subdued people is no easy task.

In his book, *Man's Search for Meaning*, Victor Frankl describes his life in a German concentration camp. Frankl was a psychiatrist by profession and Jewish in his religion. Between 1942 and 1945 he faced death each day of his life. Somehow, among the fear, uncertainty, and doubt, he found a reason for living. Each day he would ask himself the question, "What do I still have to give in spite of what has been taken from me?"

Frankl reminded himself each day that while the prison guards had almost absolute control over his life, he still had control over how he would respond to their unjust treatment. He accepted the reality that life is not fair. We do not always get treated as we think we should. There are a lot of reasons to be resentful toward those who have hurt us or wronged us in some way or another.

Haggai's message to the returning Israelites was not to give up the work that God had set before them, because the Lord God was with them. What they had been called to do, God would empower them to accomplish. They were reminded that the work belonged to God and the results belonged to God. They were called to be faithful in their work for the Lord, in spite of the challenges that lay before them. They were encouraged not to give up, because God had not given up on them. In spite of their imperfections, they would be a channel of great blessing. God would make it happen.

Fear, Uncertainty, and Doubt can paralyze God's people to the point that nothing is accomplished. If we will seek to find what we still have to offer, we may discover the power of God to accomplish some very meaningful things with what we have to offer. We can accomplish great things, because we serve a great and powerful God who works among us to bring us through our tragedies to a place where we may function, as Henri Nowen calls it, as "Wounded Healers."

Through our pain and suffering, we, too, may be agents of healing to others.

Are you willing to be a wounded healer?

YOUR BEST IS GOOD ENOUGH

It was the day that someone from the Band Room went from room to room asking the question; "Does anyone want to play in the school band?" So off I went with several of my 1st grade friends. When I was asked what instrument I wanted to play, I chose the trombone, because that's what Clara Bell on the Howdy Dowdy Show played. The response from the band leader was: "Your arms are too short; go back to your room." So that's what I did!

Many years later when I had the opportunity to be a member of a local band, I wondered if it would be a worthless effort for me to try. My first experience had been a great disappointment for a 1st grader, but I was older now, so I could handle the inevitable "No, you're not good enough." Then I heard about the band motto: "Your Best Is Good Enough." I wondered, "Are these people crazy or what? They don't have a clue how bad I am." I was convinced that until they saw me, they really did not know what deep bad looked like. But my reluctance was overcome by my desire to see what would happen if I made the attempt. Okay, that's it; I'll give the person in charge a call and see what happens.

Lyn Allman, the director of the New Horizon Band, answered the phone. I confessed that I did not have a lot of training, but that I was willing to learn. Reminding me of the motto, Lyn explained that the purpose of the band was to allow those who had some training and those with little or no training to develop whatever talent they possessed.

Drums had always interested me, but I had another problem: I did not know how to read music. "I can help you with that," was Lyn's reply.

"How are you on patience?" I asked.

"Believe me, if you want to be a part of the band, we can make it work."

The phrase, "Your Best Is Good Enough," is powerful. What it said to me, the village idiot of music, was that my skill and performance levels would be accepted by the conductor, but what about the other band members? Although I felt like a fish out of water at my first practice session, the other band members offered enthusiastic support. I decided to put my heart and soul into this endeavor and see what happened. To my surprise, I learned how to read drum music, and the other band members continued to encourage me. Then, unfortunately for me, I was diagnosed with prostate cancer. The treatment—chemotherapy, radiation therapy, and radioactive seeds—did a number on me. All in all, it was a short trip of about one year before I had to give up on this venture. I still believe strongly it was worth the experience, and I will treasure the friendships.

Not every calling or opportunity is necessarily for life. Over a period of time, we are being commissioned and de-commissioned for a certain duty, and then we move on to what's next. As Kenny Rogers informs us in one of his songs, we must know when to hold them and when to fold them, when to walk away, when to run.

When Jesus called together his dirty dozen, they brought with them a variety of talents and skills that would be of value in their pilgrimage. He took folks with no training in what He was calling them to do, and declared that He would eventually make them become fishers of humanity. They would learn from his style, words, and actions among the people. They, too, would make mistakes, but in spite of it, they were still good enough to be a part of The Galilean Band. Whatever they brought to the table, their best was good enough.

I believe God views our present circumstances and says, "Your Best Is Good Enough." God can deal with our best at whatever level it might be. Some days we may soar with eagles and on other days we may dwell among the mud turtles.

The emphasis is upon what we can become and not what we have been. God is able to look beyond our shortcomings and see what we are capable of doing and becoming. Seriously, is there any reason not to offer your life, no matter what circumstance or condition it might be in, to God, knowing that the best you have to offer is good enough for God.

Can you trust God with the best you have to offer?

YOUR CHEATING HEART

It was December of 1964, and it was snowing. This was just the right time to be outside enjoying God's gift from heaven. I decided to walk up to the local convenience store to see if anyone else was out walking around. It so happens that several of my friends were there. We decided to walk up Williams Street and eventually ended up at the home of Mr. and Mrs. Chumley. I had not been to this home before, but someone in our group knew the girls who lived there. We were welcomed into the home and soon we were playing music and just having a good time. In the kitchen, Mrs. Chumley was cooking up some of the best hamburgers in town. It seemed that no matter how many hungry teenagers showed up, everyone was always welcome. We liked this place so much that it became our hangout.

Eventually the youngest daughter, Geri, and I became good friends and then boyfriend/girlfriend. I suppose, at some point, you could say that we were going "steady," a term used to describe an exclusive relationship. I still had not stopped cruising with my friends in downtown Spartanburg, looping through local drive-in restaurants to check out the girls. On one particular evening, we met some girls from Cowpens, a nearby town. We exchanged phone numbers and pictures and made plans to meet again later on in the week.

On one particular weekend, Geri went with her parents to visit some relatives who lived in Cowpens. As she was talking with her two cousins, one of them remarked that she had a new boyfriend. He lived in Spartanburg and was attending the local technical college. Geri remarked that her boyfriend was attending that college, too. Geri's cousin had a picture of her boyfriend and as she handed the picture to Geri, she said, "His name is Bob." As Geri looked at the picture, there were feelings of mixed emotions that came over her. Yes, she knew this person in the picture. Geri exclaimed, "This is the Bob Ford I've been telling you about. We have been dating for six months."

The cat was out of the bag! I had been caught cheating on my steady girlfriend. Of all the girls in the Spartanburg area, I picked out her first cousin. Talk about bad luck! There was no way to talk my way out of this situation, but somehow we worked it out and continued to see one another as before.

At the time that Geri and I met, I was halfway through my second year at Spartanburg TEC. I graduated the following August and soon went off to serve a six-year tour in the U.S. Air Force. Since Geri had two more years in high school at the time, I felt that it was wrong for her to wait for me while I went off to serve my country during the Vietnam War. So I insisted that we no longer go steady. This decision was met with mixed emotions for both of us, but I still believed that it was the right thing to do. Later on Geri married, and eventually, I found God's person for me.

Later on in life, as a member of the Army Reserve, I was deployed to Germany as part of a backfill for the First Armored Division. One of the programs on the Armed Forces Network called "Cheaters" provided video of individuals who were suspected of cheating on their significant other. In most cases they made the video available to the person being cheated on.

It was not a pretty picture when the person being cheated on, along with the camera crew, invaded the space of the significant other in the act of cheating. Things often got down and dirty and sometimes a bit out of hand. Fortunately, there was help to break things up to prevent any serious harm from being inflicted.

The hurt and pain of the person betrayed was devastating. As the country and western song goes, "She ripped out my heart and stomped it on the floor." Some would say that it just takes time to heal from such an experience. In fact, it's not so much about time as it is how we use our time. The first step in healing is to embrace the hurt and pain. Don't deny it or ignore it. It belongs to you! Then claim whatever feelings this produces in you. It's not a sin to have certain feelings about a person who has hurt you.

Remember that being angry is not a sin; it is what we do with our anger. The scriptures tell us that we "Should not let the sun go down on our anger." In other words, don't invite anger to become a permanent part of your life. You need to find a caring person who will listen to you without trying to fix you. The process of verbalizing our feelings and emo-tions allows us to eventually come to the point where we are ready to let go and move on with our life.

It was from the Cross that Jesus uttered the words, "Father forgive them for they know not what they do." This does not mean that you become the best of friends again, but it does mean that you are ready to go on with the rest of your life.

In the "Sermon on The Mount," Jesus invites his audience to:

Come unto me, all of you that labor and are heavy laden with the concerns of this world, and I will give you rest; a peace which will blow you away.
Take my yoke, which will fit you perfectly; because I made it especially for you.
I am a meek and humble person; and in me, you will find rest for your troubled soul.
The burden that I give to you, I will empower you to carry, and it will not be too heavy for you.
Matthew 11: 27-30
(*Paraphrase by RLF*)

We can decide to live with our anger and our desire to bend, fold, and mutilate the other person, or we may choose to go from a "broken heart" to a "mended

201

heart." The Bee Gees in one of their songs ask the question, "How do you mend a broken heart?" No answer is given. Instead another question is asked: "Will you help me please?" Perhaps that is the answer to the question! There are some things that we can't do by ourselves; we need help. The Psalmist certainly seemed to understand this when he prayed; "God will you please make my heart new and clean and make my spirit strong and true deep down inside of me?" Ps. 51:10 (*Paraphrase by RLF*)

So, what is the condition of your heart?

FINDING GOD
IN UNFAMILIAR PLACES
AFTERWORD

I hope that in some way my third book, *Finding God in Unfamiliar Places*, has allowed you to discover your stories of how God's grace and mercy have touched your life. Self-discovery is often a most difficult task. We live so close to the forest that we can't see the trees. Also, we often leave stuff out of our story, because we don't think it is important enough to be included. The bits and pieces of our life that we leave on the cutting room floor may well hold the greater meaning of who we are and the nature of our destiny.

If my book has helped you discover some bits and pieces of your life that have been overlooked, then I have done my job. You may do two things to allow others to discover some of the meaning you have received. One is to write a book review. More reviews create more exposure of the book to the public. Second, just talking about the book with family and friends and co-workers would be helpful. Again thank you for reading the book and for sharing it with others.

My next books out will be *A Hobbit's View of God* and *Things Remembered*.

God's Blessings,

Robert Loran Ford

BIBLIOGRAPHY

Christ & Culture, by H. Richard Niebuhr
God of the Oppressed, by James H. Cone
Honest to God, by John A. T. Robinson
Know Your Story and Lead with It, by Richard L. Hester
and Keli Walker-Jones
Man's Search for Meaning, by Viktor E. Frankl
The Masks We Wear, by Eugene C. Rollins
The Misunderstood Jew, by Amy-Jill Levine
The Power of the Powerless, by Jurgen Moltmann
Whatever Became of Sin? by Karl Menninger

WHAT OTHERS ARE SAYING ABOUT: FINDING GOD IN UNFAMILIAR PLACES

Through everyday life stories, The Reverend Robert Loran Ford has created a powerful book, *Finding God In Unfamiliar Places*, which shows us how God's amazing Light is always within us and around us. He challenges us to discover ways to give ourselves away in service to others in order to make this world a better place to live. I have seen the stories lived out in his life as we worked together on a number of occasions in the Neonatal Intensive Care Unit at Frye Hospital. The stories from this book have been used on numerous occasions in our weekly Veterans Helping Veterans meeting to give hope and inspiration to our homeless/needy veterans. The stories have been a blessing to me, as I know they will be a blessing to you.

Eva B. Helton, RNC
Retired Neonatal Intensive Care Nurse

The master storyteller Chaplain (LTC) Robert Loran Ford invites us to sit with him as he weaves interesting and easily identifiable stories of his life's journey with familiar scripture passages and biblical figures illustrating how God is at work in the common everyday events of our world. This book is perfect for pastors in need of sermon illustrations, teachers, or anyone who is a follower of Christ. I'm so glad I took the time to pull up a chair to listen in. Believe me, you won't be disappointed.

The Reverend Sandi Hood
President of the Hickory Area Ministers
Director of Community Relations
Carolina Caring
Hickory, North Carolina

ABOUT THE AUTHOR

Robert Loran Ford was born in Ruth, North Carolina. No, Ruth, N.C., does not have a hospital with an OB/GYN Unit. In fact this small town located in the foothills of western N.C. doesn't even have a doctor's office. The birth took place in the small mill village home of Manley and Bessie Ford, the grandparents, early in the morning of December 19, 1944. He would be the first and only child of Ralph William Ford and Emma Lou Skipper Ford.

Robert grew up in the Grace Cotton Mill Village, which was located about halfway between Ruth and Rutherfordton. It was the perfect place for an only child, because there were kids all over the village. It was also one of those places where everyone knew your name.

In mid fall of 1957, Robert's family moved to Valley Falls, SC, and just about ten miles from Spartanburg.

No kids there, but within a year the family moved to 809 Farley Ave. Ext, which was located near Saxon Mill, where Ralph William Ford worked.

In the fall of 1958 Robert was enrolled at Fairforest H.S. and graduated in the class of 1963. In the summer of 1965 he graduated from Spartanburg TEC and soon after that joined the U.S. Air Force. After his tour of duty with the Air Force, Robert landed a job with Western Electric and then WSPA-TV as an engineer on top of Hogback Mountain, which was the transmitter site.

While there he was confronted with a call to a ministerial vocation. Unable to talk God out of this proposal, Robert ended up at Spartanburg Methodist College and then Gardner-Webb College. He started seminary at Golden Gate and graduated at Southeastern.

After several pastorates, Robert became the Director of Pastoral Care at FRMC in Hickory, NC. During his twenty-four years at the hospital, he finished out his tour of duty with the Army in Germany. The North Carolina Chaplains' Association bestowed upon him the Chaplain of the Year Award for 2005.

With the prompting of family and friends, Robert has attempted to put his life experiences into some devotional books. Some of the names should have been changed to protect the innocent, but that did not happen. Happy trails!

OTHER BOOKS BY
ROBERT LORAN FORD

Behind Grandma's Apron Strings

Walking in Grandpa's Footsteps

A Hobbit's View of God (To be published soon)

Don't Miss Out

Visit the website below and you may sign up to receive emails whenever Robert Loran Ford publishes a new book.

https://books2read.com/r/B-A-DUUF-GGSR

BOOKS2READ

Connecting independent readers to independent writers!

Learn more about Robert and his books
at Author Central
https://tinyurl.com/yy8bho6l

Contact Robert Loran Ford
chaplain.hobbit@gmail.com

Contact His Way Publishing:
customerservice.ebooks@gmail.com

www.ingramcontent.com/pod-product-compliance
Lightning Source LLC
LaVergne TN
LVHW051509080426
835509LV00017B/1991